INDIAN IMMIGRATION

Jan McDaniel

THE CHANGING
Face of North America:
IMMIGRATION SINCE 1965

Asylees

Chinese Immigration

Cuban Immigration

Deported Aliens

Filipino Immigration

Haitian Immigration

Immigration from Central America

Immigration from the Dominican Republic

Immigration from the Former Yugoslavia

Immigration from the Middle East

Immigration from South America

Indian Immigration

Korean Immigration

Mexican Immigration

Refugees

Vietnamese Immigration

INDIAN
IMMIGRATION

Jan McDaniel

MASON CREST PUBLISHERS
PHILADELPHIA

Produced by OTTN Publishing, Stockton, New Jersey

Mason Crest Publishers
370 Reed Road
Broomall, PA 19008
www.masoncrest.com

First printing

1 3 5 7 9 8 6 4 2

Library of Congress Cataloging-in-Publication Data

McDaniel, Jan.
  Indian immigration / Jan McDaniel.
     p. cm. — (The changing face of North America)
Summary: An overview of immigration from India to the United States and Canada since the 1960s, and particularly since the technology boom of the 1990s when highly skilled professionals came seeking better incomes and opportunities than they could find in their homeland.
Includes bibliographical references (p.) and index.
  ISBN 1-59084-683-4
1. East Indian Americans—History—20th century—Juvenile literature. 2. East Indians—Canada—History—20th century—Juvenile literature. 3. Immigrants—United States—History—20th century—Juvenile literature.
4. Immigrants—Canada—History—20th century—Juvenile literature. 5. India—Emigration and immigration—History—20th century—Juvenile literature. 6. United States—Emigration and immigration—History—20th century—Juvenile literature. 7. Canada—Emigration and immigration—History—20th century—Juvenile literature.
[1. East Indian Americans—History—20th century. 2. East Indians—Canada—History—20th century.
3. Immigrants—United States—History—20th century. 4. Immigrants—Canada—History—20th century.
5. India—Emigration and immigration—History—20th century. 6. United States—Emigration and immigration—History—20th century. 7. Canada—Emigration and immigration—History—20th century.] I. Title. II. Series.
  E184.E2M33 2004
  304.8'73054--dc22
                                                                                          2003016371

THE **Face of North America:**
IMMIGRATION SINCE 1965

CONTENTS

INTRODUCTION

THE CHANGING FACE OF AMERICA

By Senator Edward M. Kennedy

America is proud of its heritage and history as a nation of immigrants, and my own family is an example. All eight of my great-grandparents were immigrants who left Ireland a century and a half ago, when that land was devastated by the massive famine caused by the potato blight. When I was a young boy, my grandfather used to take me down to the docks in Boston and regale me with stories about the Great Famine and the waves of Irish immigrants who came to America seeking a better life. He talked of how the Irish left their marks in Boston and across the nation, enduring many hardships and harsh discrimination, but also building the railroads, digging the canals, settling the West, and filling the factories of a growing America. According to one well-known saying of the time, "under every railroad tie, an Irishman is buried."

America was the promised land for them, as it has been for so many other immigrants who have found shelter, hope, opportunity, and freedom. Immigrants have always been an indispensable part of our nation. They have contributed immensely to our communities, created new jobs and whole new industries, served in our armed forces, and helped make America the continuing land of promise that it is today.

The inspiring poem by Emma Lazarus, inscribed on the pedestal of the Statue of Liberty in New York Harbor, is America's welcome to all immigrants:

Give me your tired, your poor,
Your huddled masses yearning to breathe free,
The wretched refuse of your teeming shore,
Send these, the homeless, tempest-tossed, to me:
I lift my lamp beside the golden door.

The period since September 11, 2001, has been particularly challenging for immigrants. Since the horrifying terrorist attacks, there has been a resurgence of anti-immigrant attitudes and behavior. We all agree that our borders must be safe and secure. Yet, at the same time, we must safeguard the entry of the millions of persons who come to the United States legally each year as immigrants, visitors, scholars, students, and workers. The "golden door" must stay open. We must recognize that immigration is not the problem—terrorism is. We must identify and isolate the terrorists, and not isolate America.

One of my most important responsibilities in the Senate is the preservation of basic rights and basic fairness in the application of our immigration laws, so that new generations of immigrants in our own time and for all time will have the same opportunity that my great-grandparents had when they arrived in America.

Immigration is beneficial for the United States and for countries throughout the world. It is no coincidence that two hundred years ago, our nations' founders chose *E Pluribus Unum*—"out of many, one"—as America's motto. These words, chosen by Benjamin Franklin, John Adams, and Thomas Jefferson, refer to the ideal that separate colonies can be transformed into one united nation. Today, this ideal has come to apply to individuals as well. Our diversity is our strength. We are a nation of immigrants, and we always will be.

FOREWORD

THE CHANGING FACE OF THE UNITED STATES

Marian L. Smith, historian
U.S. Immigration and Naturalization Service

Americans commonly assume that immigration today is very different than immigration of the past. The immigrants themselves appear to be unlike immigrants of earlier eras. Their language, their dress, their food, and their ways seem strange. At times people fear too many of these new immigrants will destroy the America they know. But has anything really changed? Do new immigrants have any different effect on America than old immigrants a century ago? Is the American fear of too much immigration a new development? Do immigrants really change America more than America changes the immigrants? The very subject of immigration raises many questions.

In the United States, immigration is more than a chapter in a history book. It is a continuous thread that links the present moment to the first settlers on North American shores. From the first colonists' arrival until today, immigrants have been met by Americans who both welcomed and feared them. Immigrant contributions were always welcome—on the farm, in the fields, and in the factories. Welcoming the poor, the persecuted, and the "huddled masses" became an American principle. Beginning with the original Pilgrims' flight from religious persecution in the 1600s, through the Irish migration to escape starvation in the 1800s, to the relocation of Central Americans seeking refuge from civil wars in the 1980s and 1990s, the United States has considered itself a haven for the destitute and the oppressed.

But there was also concern that immigrants would not adopt American ways, habits, or language. Too many immigrants might overwhelm America. If so, the dream of the Founding Fathers for United States government and society would be destroyed. For this reason, throughout American history some have argued that limiting or ending immigration is our patriotic duty. Benjamin Franklin feared there were so many German immigrants in Pennsylvania the Colonial Legislature would begin speaking German. "Progressive" leaders of the early 1900s feared that immigrants who could not read and understand the English language were not only exploited by "big business," but also served as the foundation for "machine politics" that undermined the U.S. Constitution. This theme continues today, usually voiced by those who bear no malice toward immigrants but who want to preserve American ideals.

Have immigrants changed? In colonial days, when most colonists were of English descent, they considered Germans, Swiss, and French immigrants as different. They were not "one of us" because they spoke a different language. Generations later, Americans of German or French descent viewed Polish, Italian, and Russian immigrants as strange. They were not "like us" because they had a different religion, or because they did not come from a tradition of constitutional government. Recently, Americans of Polish or Italian descent have seen Nicaraguan, Pakistani, or Vietnamese immigrants as too different to be included. It has long been said of American immigration that the latest ones to arrive usually want to close the door behind them.

It is important to remember that fear of individual immigrant groups seldom lasted, and always lessened. Benjamin Franklin's anxiety over German immigrants disappeared after those immigrants' sons and daughters helped the nation gain independence in the Revolutionary War. The Irish of the mid-1800s were among the most hated immigrants, but today we all wear green on St. Patrick's Day. While a century ago it was feared that Italian and other Catholic immigrants would vote as directed by the Pope, today that controversy is only a vague memory. Unfortunately, some ethnic groups continue their efforts to earn acceptance. The African

Americans' struggle continues, and some Asian Americans, whose families have been in America for generations, are the victims of current anti-immigrant sentiment.

Time changes both immigrants and America. Each wave of new immigrants, with their strange language and habits, eventually grows old and passes away. Their American-born children speak English. The immigrants' grandchildren are completely American. The strange foods of their ancestors—spaghetti, baklava, hummus, or tofu—become common in any American restaurant or grocery store. Much of what the immigrants brought to these shores is lost, principally their language. And what is gained becomes as American as St. Patrick's Day, Hanukkah, or Cinco de Mayo, and we forget that it was once something foreign.

Recent immigrants are all around us. They come from every corner of the earth to join in the American Dream. They will continue to help make the American Dream a reality, just as all the immigrants who came before them have done.

FOREWORD

THE CHANGING FACE OF CANADA

Peter A. Hammerschmidt
First Secretary, Permanent Mission of Canada to the United Nations

Throughout Canada's history, immigration has shaped and defined the very character of Canadian society. The migration of peoples from every part of the world into Canada has profoundly changed the way we look, speak, eat, and live. Through close and distant relatives who left their lands in search of a better life, all Canadians have links to immigrant pasts. We are a nation built by and of immigrants.

Two parallel forces have shaped the history of Canadian immigration. The enormous diversity of Canada's immigrant population is the most obvious. In the beginning came the enterprising settlers of the "New World," the French and English colonists. Soon after came the Scottish, Irish, and Northern and Central European farmers of the 1700s and 1800s. As the country expanded westward during the mid-1800s, migrant workers began arriving from China, Japan, and other Asian countries. And the turbulent twentieth century brought an even greater variety of immigrants to Canada, from the Caribbean, Africa, India, and Southeast Asia.

So while English- and French-Canadians are the largest ethnic groups in the country today, neither group alone represents a majority of the population. A large and vibrant multicultural mix makes up the rest, particularly in Canada's major cities. Toronto, Vancouver, and Montreal alone are home to people from over 200 ethnic groups!

Less obvious but equally important in the evolution of Canadian immigration has been hope. The promise of a better life lured Europeans and Americans seeking cheap (sometimes even free) farmland. Thousands of Scots and Irish arrived to escape grinding poverty and starvation. Others came for freedom, to escape religious and political persecution. Canada has long been a haven to the world's dispossessed and disenfranchised—Dutch and German farmers cast out for their religious beliefs, black slaves fleeing the United States, and political refugees of despotic regimes in Europe, Africa, Asia, and South America.

The two forces of diversity and hope, so central to Canada's past, also shaped the modern era of Canadian immigration. Following the Second World War, Canada drew heavily on these influences to forge trailblazing immigration initiatives.

The catalyst for change was the adoption of the Canadian Bill of Rights in 1960. Recognizing its growing diversity and Canadians' changing attitudes towards racism, the government passed a federal statute barring discrimination on the grounds of race, national origin, color, religion, or sex. Effectively rejecting the discriminatory elements in Canadian immigration policy, the Bill of Rights forced the introduction of a new policy in 1962. The focus of immigration abruptly switched from national origin to the individual's potential contribution to Canadian society. The door to Canada was now open to every corner of the world.

Welcoming those seeking new hopes in a new land has also been a feature of Canadian immigration in the modern era. The focus on economic immigration has increased along with Canada's steadily growing economy, but political immigration has also been encouraged. Since 1945, Canada has admitted tens of thousands of displaced persons, including Jewish Holocaust survivors, victims of Soviet crackdowns in Hungary and Czechoslovakia, and refugees from political upheaval in Uganda, Chile, and Vietnam.

Prior to 1978, however, these political refugees were admitted as an exception to normal immigration procedures. That year, Canada revamped its refugee policy with a new Immigration Act that explicit-ly affirmed Canada's commitment to the resettlement of refugees from oppression. Today, the admission of refugees remains a central part of Canadian immigration law and regulations.

Amendments to economic and political immigration policy continued during the 1980s and 1990s, refining further the bold steps taken during the modern era. Together, these initiatives have turned Canada into one of the world's few truly multicultural states.

Unlike the process of assimilation into a "melting pot" of cultures, immigrants to Canada are more likely to retain their cultural identity, beliefs, and practices. This is the source of some of Canada's greatest strengths as a society. And as a truly multicultural nation, diversity is not seen as a threat to Canadian identity. Quite the contrary—diversity *is* Canadian identity.

1 INDIANS IN NORTH AMERICA

Indian immigrants enrich North American society with their culture, economic and intellectual productivity, strong family values, and work ethics. Most believe they will get ahead by working hard and persevering at whatever they do. Some have succeeded to the point of becoming millionaires, and even billionaires, using equal shares of self-discipline and daring.

Indians and Indian Americans (first- and second-generation immigrants and those descended from immigrants who came a long time ago) make up approximately 0.6 percent of the U.S. population, according to the 2000 census. The U.S. Indian population as of the 2000 census was 1,678,765, a total nearly equal to the population of the state of Nebraska. This total represents an increase of 106 percent from the 815,447 people of Indian descent reported to be living in the United States in 1990. As of the 2001 Canadian census there were 314,690 Indians, or about 1 percent of Canada's national population, which was approximately 30 million.

These immigrants arriving to North America have traveled thousands of miles from their homeland, the Republic of India, which occupies a little less than 1.3 million square miles (3,287,590 square kilometers) of southern Asia. India is bordered on the west by the Arabian Sea and Pakistan; on the north by China, Nepal, and Bhutan; and on the east by the Bay of Bengal, Bangladesh, and Myanmar (formerly known as Burma). Just over one-third the size of the United States, India

◀A growing number of Indians are leaving their homes in South Asia to resettle in North America. Indian Americans fall behind the Filipinos and the Chinese in population size, but they comprise the fastest-growing Asian American group, with an annual growth rate of 7.6 percent. In Canada, Indians are the largest immigrant group behind the Chinese.

Hinduism in North America

In 1893, 30-year-old Hindu Swami Vivekananda (1863–1902) introduced North Americans to the Hindu religion and yoga. Arriving as a missionary dressed in turban and robes, he addressed the World Parliament of Religions at the 1893 Chicago Columbia Exposition. All world religions were supposed to be represented at the fair, yet no Hindu had been invited, and the swami was nearly prohibited from speaking. But once he stepped on stage and addressed the audience, he received a standing ovation. Vivekananda discussed religious tolerance and unity, a theme he continued to expound upon over the next seven years of his lecturing in the United States and Britain.

The swami preached the Vedanta philosophy, a Hindu set of fundamental principles maintaining that all religious traditions are equal and man's true nature is divine. Vivekananda founded the Vedanta Society, which operates 20 ashrams, or spiritual centers, in the United States, as well as one in Canada. Traditionally, membership has been white, but more Indians have joined following the increase in immigration during the 1990s.

Hindu immigrants make up half of New York City's Vedanta Society membership. The society runs summer camps where Hindu children socialize with kids of similar backgrounds. They are exposed to religious beliefs, values, and traditions and learn how to chant prayers, feel comfortable in a temple, and practice yoga. Hinduism has become the world's third-largest religion, behind Christianity and Islam. More than one million of an estimated 850 million Hindus worldwide live in the United States.

is home to over a billion people. More than three-quarters of the population practice the Hindu faith.

Indians generally come to North America in search of better professional opportunities and a better life for their children, though a small segment of the population is escaping persecution or dangerous conditions. Although the number of Indians in North America is only a small percentage of the overall population, the Indian population is growing rapidly. In fact, its average annual growth rate of 7.6 percent is the largest of all the Asian American groups. Indians make up 16.4 percent of the Asian American community in North America, forming the third-largest group behind the Chinese and Filipinos.

The United States welcomed 71,105 immigrants from India in 2002, according to the *Yearbook of Immigration Statistics* of that year. In 2001, the Canadian census reported that Canada opened its doors to 27,812 Indians, making them the second-largest immigrant group behind the Chinese.

The Typical Immigrant

Most Indian immigrants are middle or upper class, well educated, and English-speaking. According to a March 2000 report by the Embassy of India in Washington, D.C., more than 87 percent of Indian immigrants in the U.S. have a high school diploma, and some 62 to 75 percent hold at least a bachelor's degree (compared with the 21 percent of the overall U.S. population who hold a bachelor's degree, as reported in a 2002 study based on U.S. Census data). Even many of those Indians lacking the formal education of the immigrant group's majority have had success buying or starting up thriving businesses.

The economic status that Indian Americans have reached is a good indicator of their success. Their annual buying power is estimated at $20 billion, and their per capita income is more than twice that of the general population. The Embassy of India reported that the median family income of Indians in the U.S. was $60,093 in 2000, compared to the national family median income of $38,885.

In 2000, three-quarters of all Indian Americans were employed, as reported by the Embassy of India. Almost half of them work in management or professional occupations and a third in technical, sales, and administrative positions. About 300,000 work in the San Jose–Palo Alto area of California, better known as "Silicon Valley," where technology jobs offer a median income of around $125,000 a year. More than 5,000 Indian Americans are faculty members of colleges and universities. According to a June 2000 report in *Time Select/Global Business Report* magazine, only 6 percent of Indian immigrants

live in poverty. Fewer than 1 percent receive public assistance.

In 2002 there were more Indian students in the U.S. than any other foreign student group in the country. A 2002 report called *Open Doors*, a publication of the Institute of International Education, stated there were 66,836 Indian students enrolled in U.S. schools—about 12 percent of the foreign student population. According to Citizenship and Immigration Canada (CIC), the number of Indian students in Canada increased about 30 percent in 2001 to a total of 1,226.

Indian Influence on Western Culture

The presence of Indians in North America has exposed Westerners to a variety of cultural traditions, ranging from food and fashion to philosophies on religion and health.

Today, most North American cities and towns have Indian restaurants. They offer a variety of traditional foods, many of them vegetarian (prepared without meat). One popular dish,

A typical Indian meal served at a restaurant in Los Angeles, California. One outcome of the increased immigration from India is the growing popularity of Indian cuisine in the United States and Canada. Indian restaurants can be found in most cities.

navratan korma, consists of five vegetables in a cream sauce, cooked by the *Balti* method. The word *Balti* refers to the large pot in which the food is cooked over high heat. Other popular Indian foods include *tandoori* chicken, chicken curry, and *nan*, Indian flat bread.

Trendy coffeehouses such as Starbucks serve the Indian drink *chai*, a strong and heavily spiced tea. According to legend, *chai* was created for a king in India who thought it was such a luxury that he would not allow it to be served outside his court. The blend of black teas is seasoned with cinnamon, cardamom, cloves, ginger, nutmeg, honey, and milk. Coffeehouses serve it iced or hot with a cinnamon stick or whipped cream. Health food stores sell *chai* in liquid concentrate, powder mix, or loose tea form.

Many Westerners have adopted Indian fashion, in a number of cases for the sake of fun and style and not for its religious or cultural significance. For example, during the 1990s, the

Bringing India to America

Children's writer Dhan Gopal Mukerji (1890–1936) arrived in the United States penniless in 1910. To pay his tuition at the University of California, he took menial jobs and unskilled farm and factory work.

Mukerji worked his way to become the first South Asian immigrant with a successful literary career, writing books that wove together Indian lore, culture, and religion. In 1928, he became the first Asian and only Indian to win the American Library Association's prestigious Newbery Medal for children's literature. He received the award for his 1927 book *Gay Neck: the Story of a Pigeon*, which was based on his childhood experiences in Calcutta. Mukerji wrote nine children's books of animal stories, including *Kari the Elephant*, in 1922, and *Ghond the Hunter*, in 1928.

The author's total output includes more than 20 books spanning fiction, nonfiction, poetry, drama, and translations. Mukerji's 1923 biography, *Caste and Outcast*, introduced many Americans to India's landscape and culture. The book contrasts Hindu spirituality and life in India with the materialism of the West. It has been reprinted and translated many times.

One Indian traditional fashion that has found particular favor among Americans and Canadians is *mehndi*, an elaborate style of semi-permanent markings applied on the hands and other parts of the body. *Mehndi* particularly became a fashionable trend among non-Indians during the 1990s. In traditional Indian households, *mehndi* designs are placed on a bride in preparation for marriage.

"Indo-chic" trend became popular. T-shirts portrayed images of Hindu gods. Westerners sported *mehndi*, elaborate tattoos made from a special paste called henna—in Indian tradition *mehndi* designs are placed on a bride in preparation for marriage. American beauty salons applied elaborate semi-permanent designs. Celebrities popularized the wearing of the *bindi*, a distinctive round red dot worn by Indian brides. In keeping with the *bindis* style, Westerners also placed self-stick gemstones on their foreheads. In the late 1990s, these gemstones moved to other parts of the body with stenciled designs painted around them.

With the growth of the Indian immigrant population has also come much exposure of Hindu beliefs and philosophies to Westerners. In the 1970s Maharishi Mahesh Yogi, a guru to the famous rock group the Beatles, introduced ayurveda to the United States. Ayurveda, the Hindu science of life, comes from the Sanskrit words for "life" and "knowledge." (Sanskrit is the ancient sacred and literary language of India.) The word *ayurveda* literally means "wisdom of life," and has been a major philosophy and medical system throughout Indian history, handed down orally and through Sanskrit poetry.

To ensure one's health, well-being, and longevity, ayurveda emphasizes harmony between mind, body, and spirit. The basic beliefs of ayurveda establish three underlying *doshas*, or mind-body principles—*kapha*, *vata*, and *pitta*. From birth, the *doshas* are in force, influencing human traits ranging from skin type to personality. Balancing all three *doshas* through meditation, nutrition, exercise, herbal formulas, surgery, and yoga ensures health and beauty.

Ayurveda has become a commercial success in America, with the opening of ayurvedic spas and the marketing of a variety of ayurvedic products made from Indian oils and herbs. Ayurvedic herbal compounds are used in the manufacture of some lip protectors and sunscreens.

Yoga is based on the ancient principle that the body is the temple of the spirit. A popular form of exercise, yoga attributes good health to spiritual growth through stress reduction. Growing numbers of yoga classes are taught today in neighborhood YMCAs and community centers.

Maharishi Mahesh Yogi has been a longtime spokesman of ayurveda, a Hindu science that has attracted many American practitioners since the 1970s. Among the key practices of ayurveda, which means "science of life," are meditation and yoga, a type of exercise that has gained unheralded popularity in the United States and other Western countries.

2 INDEPENDENCE AND CONFLICT

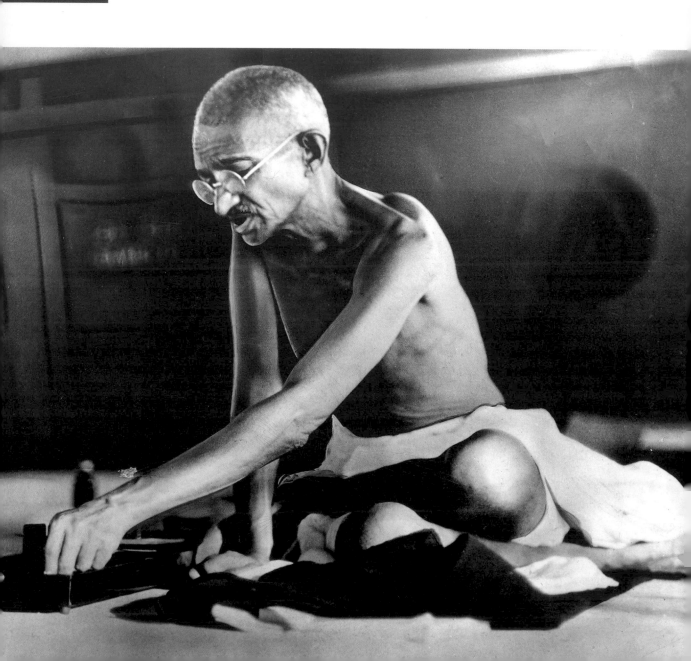

India is a complex country of contrasts. It is home to the very rich and the very poor, the well educated and the illiterate. Its cities boast advanced technology while its villages lack basic utilities. Birthplace of leader Mohandas Gandhi, who advocated change through nonviolent resistance, the country has seen a great deal of progress since achieving independence in 1947. However, India has also had great difficulty in keeping pace economically, and in recent decades has experienced riots and acts of terrorism.

The history of India dates back many centuries. Known as Bharat in ancient times, the Indus River Valley was invaded by Aryan tribes around 1500 B.C. The resulting merger of the Aryan and native civilizations gave birth to classical Indian culture and the Hindu religion. (Today, about 72 percent of India's population is Indo-Aryan, according to the U.S. State Department.) In the 10th and 11th centuries, invading Turks and Afghans brought the Islamic faith to India, which became popular among many Indians.

Around 1619, the British-owned East India Company began setting up trading stations throughout the country. By the 1850s, Great Britain controlled most of present-day India, Pakistan, and Bangladesh. Modern India's culture, educational institutions, and government reflect the years of British influence. In the early 1920s, Gandhi, an outspoken spiritual leader, led a movement against the British that eventually led to India

◀ Spiritual and political leader Mohandas Gandhi (1869–1948) led India toward gaining independence after nearly three and a half centuries of British colonial rule. Gandhi also was a vocal critic of India's oppressive caste system.

winning its independence in August 1947.

India's constitution, adopted in January 1950, established a federal government modeled on Great Britain's parliamentary system. India's democracy is similar to the U.S. system but gives the central government more power over individual states.

Language and People

Hindi is the most widely spoken language of India. Some 200 million well-educated Indians speak fluent English, which is the language used in the country's political and business worlds. India recognizes 14 other official languages, although more than 1,500 languages and dialects are spoken.

Some 30 percent of the population lives in 200 cities and towns. These include the capital, New Delhi, with a population of 11 million; Mumbai (formerly called Bombay), a western seaport and India's largest city, with a population of 15 mil-

Pandit Jawaharlal Nehru (facing camera), India's first prime minister, confers with other Indian leaders at a meeting of the Constituent Assembly in 1947. The efforts of Nehru and other Indian leaders led to the adoption of a national constitution in January 1950, which officially made India a sovereign republic.

lion; and the eastern port of Calcutta, with a population of 12 million. The other 70 percent of the population consists mostly of farmers, who live in over 550,000 rural villages scattered through the country. India's modern cities of high-rise buildings and quality schools stand in stark contrast to its poorer villages, which may lack electricity, running water, and telephone service.

On May 11, 2000, India saw the birth of its billionth citizen, baby girl Astha, meaning "Faith" in Hindi. According to the Central Intelligence Agency (CIA), as of July 2002 the Indian population totaled 1,045,845,226 people, more than 15 percent of the world's population. The country's population inhabits a land area that only occupies 2.4 percent of the world's

Located in the city of Mumbai, the Victoria Terminus train station is a symbol of India's complex history, as it demonstrates the fusion of British and Indian architectural styles. The construction of the station was completed in 1887.

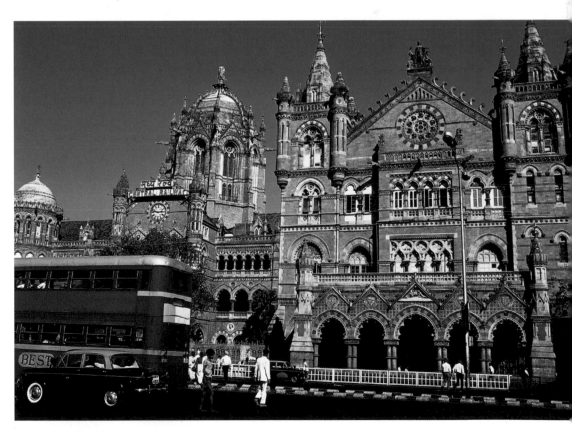

land area. The only country in the world with more people is China, which has almost 1.3 billion citizens.

A Land of Many Faiths

Hindus and Muslims constitute the largest religious groups in India. Some 80 percent of the country's population, or 700 million people, are Hindu. Twelve to 15 percent are Muslims. Estimated to number from 120 to 150 million, they make up the world's second-largest Muslim community outside Indonesia. There are 16 million Roman Catholic Indians out of a total population of 24 million Christians. The rest of the country's population is Sikh, Jain, Buddhist, or Parsi.

In India, religion, language, and—for Hindus—caste are determining factors of an individual's social position, education, career, and future. The Hindu caste system encompasses four categories: priest or scholar, warrior, merchant, and laborer. Within these categories are thousands of castes and subcastes. Being born into a certain caste can limit someone's opportunities since the

A Muslim kneels in prayer in the town of Srinagar, India. Muslims comprise 12 to 15 percent of the total Indian population, which also includes followers of the Sikh, Jain, Buddhist, Parsi, Christian, and Hindu faiths.

system dictates that jobs and social status be assigned at birth. Entire villages may be segregated by caste.

Outcasts, or "untouchables," rank at the bottom of the system. Gandhi, an opponent of the caste system, called members of this caste "Harijan" (children of God). Today they prefer to be known today as *Dalits*, the Hindi word meaning "the oppressed." About 16 percent of India's population, or an estimated 160 million people, are Dalits. They have no access to education and are forbidden to drink at wells of the upper caste or worship at their temples. Their life's work usually involves tasks considered religiously impure by the higher classes, such as cleaning toilets or handling animal carcasses. While some Dalits have escaped the social system, advancement is extremely difficult, especially in villages. Dalits may blend into the anonymity of larger cities or convert to other religions.

In 1950 the government outlawed the caste system, and provided agricultural subsidies and scholarships to untouchables. Although laws prohibit discrimination and slots are reserved for Dalits in parliament, state legislatures, government offices, and schools, the laws are not always followed and the caste system remains resistant to change.

Conflicts Between Social and Religious Factions

Muslims and Hindus have proven capable of living peacefully as neighbors, but the goal of multicultural tolerance has not always been achieved. Recent years have seen the rise of many religious, militant, and separatist organizations and an escalation of violence. While most Indians and India's government condemn the violence, riotous outbreaks and retaliatory attacks continue.

Hindu nationalism, a movement based on the belief that Hindus come first and all other groups are secondary, has been rising since the late 1980s. The Hindu nationalist Bharatiya Janata Party, led by Prime Minister Atal Bihari Vajpayee, came into power in March 1998. In a move upheld by India's supreme court, Hindu nationalists are rewriting school history texts from their perspective. New editions of books delete references to such historical truths as the 1948 assassination of Gandhi by a Hindu extremist, the oppressive effects of the caste system, and the Hindus' criticisms of certain ethnic groups and religious leaders.

For over a century the small town of Ayodhya, located in the state of Uttar Pradesh, has been the scene of violent altercations between Muslims and Hindus. The beginning of the friction dates back to 1528, the year when Muslim Emperor Mir Baqi dismantled an 11th-century Hindu temple marking what some believed to be the birthplace of the Hindu god Rama. The emperor had the Babri Mosque constructed over the site. Hindus and Muslims continued to dispute the site's rightful ownership. Rioting broke out in 1855, and 75 people died in the violence.

Subsequent riots in 1934 damaged the mosque, which was later repaired. After Hindus raided and took over the mosque in December 1949, the government locked up the building and declared it off limits. The following year, Hindus and Muslims both petitioned the courts for possession. After over three decades the mosque reopened in 1986; during the same time ground-

Atal Bihari Vajpayee was elected India's prime minister in March 1998. Vajpayee has stirred up controversy by remaining loyal to the interests of his Bharatiya Janata Party, a Hindu nationalist group that first gained major political influence in the late 1980s.

An Indian police-man surveys the burnt wreckage of the Sabarmati Express, a train that was bombed by a Muslim mob in Godhra, February 2002. A total of 58 Hindu pilgrims died in the attack, one of many attacks in a feud between the region's Hindus and Muslims that has lasted nearly 500 years.

breaking ceremonies were held for a Hindu temple to be built adjacent to the mosque. Riots broke out shortly afterward, during which 600 people died. Hundreds were killed in another outburst that occurred in 1990.

In December 1992 the conflict was re-ignited, as a mob of 4,000 Hindus, using their bare hands, pickaxes, metal rods, and sledgehammers, destroyed the 464-year-old mosque in just nine hours. After police finally drove away the attackers with stakes and tear gas, the mob then decided to destroy other Muslim structures, looting and burning about 270 Muslim homes and destroying 18 other local mosques. Eventually, riot-ing spread to at least 1,000 villages throughout India, Pakistan, and Bangladesh. More than 1,100 were dead and 4,000 injured. Hindu temples were destroyed. Hundreds more per-ished in subsequent rioting that erupted in Mumbai.

Hindu-Muslim hostilities continued to simmer, erupting again 10 years later. In February 2002, the Sabarmati Express, a train

Conflict with Pakistan

A longstanding disagreement between the governments of India and Pakistan deepened into a crisis in January 2002, when tens of thousands of Indian and Pakistani troops faced off. This clash was particularly unnerving to international leaders because both countries had nuclear capability, making war potentially more catastrophic than usual. To help ease tensions, U.S. Secretary of State Colin Powell visited both countries and held discussions with their leaders. Pakistan's roundup of hundreds of Islamic militants during that month helped establish a tentative truce that prevented imminent war.

The most immediate source of the crisis was India's accusation that Pakistan supported the separatist movement in the Indian state of Kashmir. In 2001 the Kashmiri separatists attacked the state assembly building and India's Parliament complex. Yet even before this conflict, hostilities existed between India and Pakistan as early as Britain's decision to form the two independent countries in 1947. The British, upon leaving India, thought they could diminish tensions between Hindus and Muslims by partitioning the country, creating the separate Muslim state of Pakistan. An estimated 12.5 million people were uprooted, as religious groups were assigned places to live—Hindus in India and Muslims in Pakistan.

The result was one of the world's largest migrations. After tossing aside belongings they could not carry with them, herds of desperate people walked hundreds of miles in the brutal heat. Many were too frail from age or illness to make the journey and died. Meanwhile, Hindu-Muslim violence continued to break out, especially in Punjab. People were beaten to death with clubs and stones. Over four months, an estimated 500,000 to 1 million people were killed.

India and Pakistan continued to dispute borders and other issues. Both claimed rights over the states of Jammu and Kashmir, located in the northwest corner of India and bordered by China, Afghanistan, and Pakistan. Although 1947 partition boundaries placed this region that was predominantly Muslim in Pakistan, the Hindu ruler decided to align with India. When Kashmir's Muslims revolted, he agreed to surrender the state to India's control in return for military help.

India and Pakistan fought for Kashmir through January 1949, at which time the United Nations mediated a truce. Peace negotiations continued unsuccessfully through 1954. Pakistan controlled a portion of the region called Azad Kashmir. India controlled the rest and annexed it in 1957. Fighting erupted again in August 1965 when armed Pakistanis disguised as civilians slipped across the border into Indian territory. After weeks of battles that included air attacks on Indian

At a demonstration in June 1999, members of Jamaat-i-Islami, a fundamentalist Islamic party in Pakistan, condemn India's crackdown on Kashmiri militants. The support that Kashmiri separatists have received from Jammaat-i-Islami and other Islamic parties has led to increased hostilities between India and Pakistan.

and Pakistani cities, the United Nations and individual Western countries helped negotiate a cease-fire. The dispute over Kashmir and Jammu remains unresolved.

Pollution, Natural Catastrophe, and Poverty

Today, Indians along the country's disputed borders, as well as those far removed from them, face great challenges. India has had numerous weather catastrophes. A 1999 New Delhi heat wave killed hundreds, while thousands more died from cases of gastroenteritis and cholera (brought on from drinking contaminated water). In 1998 and 1999, droughts in the state of Orissa killed 2,000 people. In the summer of 2002, central and southern India suffered its worst drought in years, while at the same time in the northeastern region monsoon floods killed more than 300 people.

Apart from its natural threats, India is faced with long-standing pollution issues and infrastructure crises. Several

An Indian farmer living in the northern state of Haryana sits in his dried-out paddy field during a drought in the summer of 2002. In addition to droughts, Indians regularly face other weather catastrophes such as heat waves and monsoon flooding.

factors combine to make the residential zones of India's cities unappealing. Mumbai's slums are the largest of Asia, and half the population lacks running water. In Mumbai, as in most of India's largest cities, open cooking fires, auto rickshaws (covered two-wheeled vehicles), taxis, diesel buses, and coal-fired power plants pollute the air. A large number of Indians ride gasoline- and oil-powered motor scooters, which produce more smog than automobiles. The bad air causes sore throats and allergies. In 1996, the Australian Cricket board dropped New Delhi as a destination for future tours after Australian cricket players complained of eye and respiratory problems.

In some parts of India the water is undrinkable because raw sewage, industrial waste, and the runoff of agricultural pesticides have polluted the rivers. In heavily farmed areas, deforestation and overgrazing have caused soil erosion and desert-like conditions.

Although India's education system produces a segment of well-educated people, many never receive the instruction they need. The government provides free public education, with the requirement that students attend school through age 14, yet hundreds of thousands of children complete less than five years before dropping out. With child labor legal in India, some 100 million children under 14 are working. Almost half the people over the age of 15 are illiterate (unable to read and write). About 56 percent of the men are literate, while only 38 percent of the women can read and write. In some regions, women receive no education, and in the state of Rajasthan only about 5 percent of the women are literate.

With the world's 13th-largest gross national product (GNP), India is not a poor country overall. The annual gross national income per person is $2,500, and there is a growing middle class of 150 to 200 million. However, a wide gap divides the rich and the poor. According to an October 2002 story for the PBS news program *Frontline/World*, more than 25 percent of the population lives below the poverty line. Some 350 million

An Indian child carries bricks to a kiln in Raichak, a city 30 miles (48 km) south of Calcutta. Child labor is legal in India, and as a result, children who do not have the opportunity to attend school may be employed full-time and work under grueling conditions.

Indians survive on less than $1 per day, and only one in four has access to sanitation. The very poor lack the resources to leave India.

Technology Exporter

A sizable number of those Indians who do receive a good education hail from, or set up business in, the city of Bangalore. The capital of the state of Karnataka, Bangalore is known as India's "Silicon State." Home to advanced high-technology firms, it is a city of high-rises and plush modern office complexes. In 2000, colleges in Bangalore were reported to turn out 30,000 engineering graduates per year. Limited opportunities in India have made the country a major exporter of computer and technical workers. An information technology job pays about $1,000 per month in India, compared to the $50,000 or more per year that many tech companies pay their employees in North America.

Today India also exports services that are delivered by telephone and the Internet. These services include accounting, telemarketing, helpdesk support, medical transcription, payroll management, claims processing, credit evaluation services, engineering design, animation, and maintaining databases. With a skilled and English-speaking labor force that works for lower wages, Indian companies undercut competitors by 30 to 40 percent, according to a Reuters business report delivered in December 2001. Operators who speak English with an American or neutral accent are trained in American culture and adopt American names so that callers often do not realize they are speaking to someone outside the United States. More than half of America's Fortune 500 companies have contracted Indian technology support. India's revenues from such services are expected to reach an estimated $16.94 billion by 2008, according to the Reuters report.

Akashata Joshi, a representative of a delegation of Indian college students, speaks at a conference in Bombay in July 2003. Joshi belongs to the minority of women in India who receive a complete education.

3 IMMIGRATION TO NORTH AMERICA

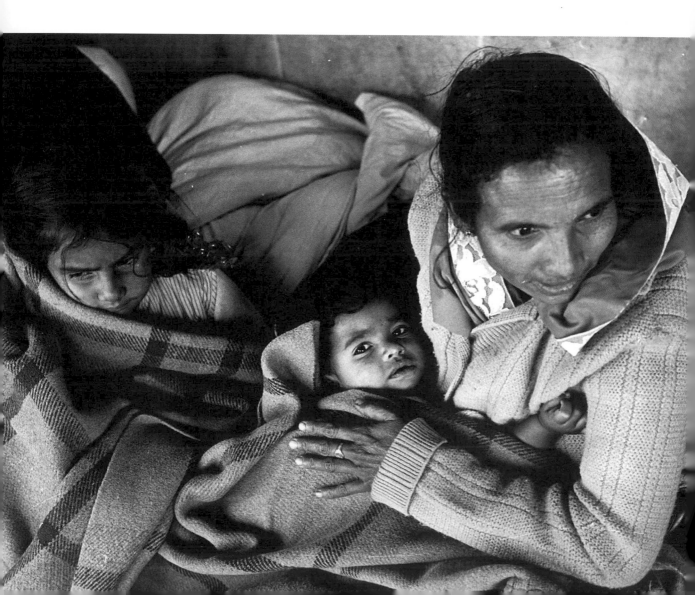

Often referred to as a "nation of immigrants," the United States has become a popular destination for Indian immigrants. The same is true for Canada—especially in recent years, as Indians have become one of the largest immigrant groups. In both countries, there has been a gradual historic move toward an "open-door" immigration policy regarding Indians. However, there have also been periods when the reception of Indian immigrants has been cooler than in other years. To have a better understanding of what has caused these changes in policy, it is important to briefly examine the history of immigration to North America.

A Short History of U.S. Immigration

Immigration to the United States has been characterized by openness punctuated by periods of restriction. During the 17th, 18th, and 19th centuries, immigration was essentially open without restriction, and, at times, immigrants were even recruited to come to America. Between 1783 and 1820, approximately 250,000 immigrants arrived at U.S. shores. Between 1841 and 1860, more than 4 million immigrants came; most were from England, Ireland, and Germany.

Historically, race and ethnicity have played a role in legislation to restrict immigration. The Chinese Exclusion Act of 1882, which was not repealed until 1943, specifically prevented Chinese people from becoming U.S. citizens and did not

◀An Asian immigrant mother waits in an airport with her two children. Before the 1960s, restrictive quotas and the great distance between South Asia and North America resulted in low immigration numbers from India. Since the important legislative acts of that decade, however, immigration has been more open, and the Indian American and Indian Canadian population has grown dramatically.

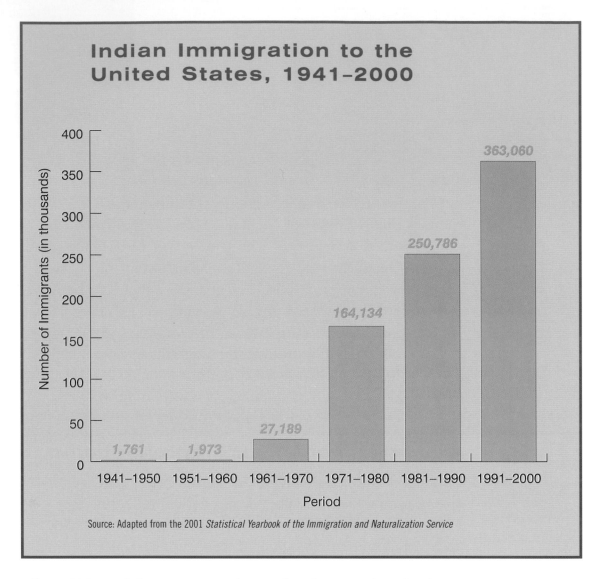

Indian Immigration to the United States, 1941–2000

Number of Immigrants (in thousands)

Period	
1941–1950	1,761
1951–1960	1,973
1961–1970	27,189
1971–1980	164,134
1981–1990	250,786
1991–2000	363,060

Period

Source: Adapted from the 2001 *Statistical Yearbook of the Immigration and Naturalization Service*

allow Chinese laborers to immigrate for the next decade. An agreement with Japan in the early 1900s prevented most Japanese immigration to the United States.

Until the 1920s, no numerical restrictions on immigration existed in the United States, although health restrictions applied. The only other significant restrictions came in 1917, when passing a literacy test became a requirement for immigrants. Presidents Cleveland, Taft, and Wilson had vetoed similar measures earlier. In addition, in 1917 a prohibition was added to the law against the immigration of people from Asia (defined as the Asiatic barred zone). While a few of these prohibitions were lifted during World War II, they were not repealed until 1952, and even then Asians were only allowed in under very small annual quotas.

U.S. Immigration Policy from World War I to 1965

During World War I, the federal government required that all travelers to the United States obtain a visa at a U.S. consulate or diplomatic post abroad. As former State Department consular affairs officer C. D. Scully points out, by making that requirement permanent Congress, by 1924, established the framework of temporary, or non-immigrant visas (for study, work, or travel), and immigrant visas (for permanent residence). That framework remains in place today.

After World War I, cultural intolerance and bizarre racial theories led to new immigration restrictions. The House Judiciary Committee employed a eugenics consultant, Dr. Harry N. Laughlin, who asserted that certain races were inferior. Another leader of the eugenics movement,

A satirical cartoon entitled "A Statue for *Our* Harbor," printed in an 1881 issue of the San Francisco–based magazine *The Wasp*, represents the anti-immigration perspective of many Americans during the 19th century. The cartoon attributes a number of social problems, including immorality, disease, filth, and the ruin of "white labor," to Chinese immigrants. The drawing appeared a year before Congress passed the Chinese Exclusion Act of 1882, which prohibited the Chinese from immigrating to the United States.

Madison Grant, argued that Jews, Italians, and others were inferior because of their supposedly different skull size.

The Immigration Act of 1924, preceded by the Temporary Quota Act of 1921, set new numerical limits on immigration based on "national origin." Taking effect in 1929, the 1924 act set annual quotas on immigrants that were specifically designed to keep out southern Europeans, such as Italians and Greeks. Generally no more than 100 people of the proscribed nationalities were permitted to immigrate.

While the new law was rigid, the U.S. Department of State's restrictive interpretation directed consular officers overseas to be even stricter in their application of the "public charge" provision. (A public charge is someone unable to support himself or his family.) As author Laura Fermi wrote, "In response to the new cry for restriction at the beginning of the [Great Depression] . . . the consuls were to interpret very strictly the clause prohibiting admission of aliens 'likely to become public

The 1965 Immigration and Nationality Act, signed by President Lyndon Johnson, was one of the century's most significant immigration acts. With its employment preferences and priorities granted to family members, the act created resettlement opportunities for thousands of newcomers from India and other Asian countries.

charges; and to deny the visa to an applicant who in their opinion might become a public charge at any time.'"

In the early 1900s, more than one million immigrants a year came to the United States. In 1930—the first year of the national-origin quotas—approximately 241,700 immigrants were admitted. But under the State Department's strict interpretations, only 23,068 immigrants entered during 1933, the smallest total since 1831. Later these restrictions prevented many Jews in Germany and elsewhere in Europe from escaping what would become the Holocaust. At the height of the Holocaust in 1943, the United States admitted fewer than 6,000 refugees.

The Displaced Persons Act of 1948, the nation's first refugee law, allowed many refugees from World War II to settle in the United States. The law put into place policy changes that had already seen immigration rise from 38,119 in 1945 to 108,721 in 1946 (and later to 249,187 in 1950). One-third of those admitted between 1948 and 1951 were Poles, with ethnic Germans forming the second-largest group.

The 1952 Immigration and Nationality Act is best known for its restrictions against those who supported communism or anarchy. However, the bill's other provisions were quite restrictive and were passed over the veto of President Truman. The 1952 act retained the national-origin quota system for the Eastern Hemisphere. The Western Hemisphere continued to operate without a quota and relied on other qualitative factors to limit immigration. Moreover, during that time, the Mexican bracero program, from 1942 to 1964, allowed millions of Mexican agricultural workers to work temporarily in the United States.

The 1952 act set aside half of each national quota to be divided among three preference categories for relatives of U.S. citizens and permanent residents. The other half went to aliens with high education or exceptional abilities. These quotas applied only to those from the Eastern Hemisphere.

A Halt to the National-Origin Quotas

The Immigration and Nationality Act of 1965 became a landmark in immigration legislation by specifically striking the racially based national-origin quotas. It removed the barriers to Asian immigration, which later led to opportunities to immigrate for many Filipinos, Chinese, Koreans, and others. The Western Hemisphere was designated a ceiling of 120,000 immigrants but without a preference system or per country limits. Modifications made in 1978 ultimately combined the Western and Eastern Hemispheres into one preference system and one ceiling of 290,000.

The 1965 act built on the existing system—without the national-origin quotas—and gave somewhat more priority to family relationships. It did not completely overturn the existing system but rather carried forward essentially intact the family immigration categories from the 1959 amendments to the Immigration and Nationality Act. Even though the text of the law prior to 1965 indicated that half of the immigration slots were reserved for skilled employment immigration, in practice, Immigration and Naturalization Service (INS) statistics show that 86 percent of the visas issued between 1952 and 1965 went for family immigration.

A number of significant pieces of legislation since 1980 have shaped the current U.S. immigration system. First, the Refugee Act of 1980 removed refugees from the annual world limit and established that the president would set the number of refugees who could be admitted each year after consultations with Congress.

Second, the 1986 Immigration Reform and Control Act (IRCA) introduced sanctions against employers who "knowingly" hired undocumented immigrants (those here illegally). It also provided amnesty for many undocumented immigrants.

Third, the Immigration Act of 1990 increased legal immigration by 40 percent. In particular, the act significantly increased the number of employment-based immigrants (to 140,000), while also boosting family immigration.

Fourth, the 1996 Illegal Immigration Reform and Immigrant Responsibility Act (IIRAIRA) significantly tightened rules that permitted undocumented immigrants to convert to legal status and made other changes that tightened immigration law in areas such as political asylum and deportation.

Fifth, in response to the September 11, 2001, terrorist attacks, the USA PATRIOT Act and the Enhanced Border Security and Visa Entry Reform Act tightened rules on the granting of visas to individuals from certain countries and enhanced the federal government's monitoring and detention authority over foreign nationals in the United States.

New U.S. Immigration Agencies

In a dramatic reorganization of the federal government, the Homeland Security Act of 2002 abolished the Immigration and Naturalization Service and transferred its immigration service and enforcement functions from the Department of Justice into a new Department of Homeland Security. The Customs Service, the Coast Guard, and parts of other agencies were also transferred into the new department.

President Bush signs the Enhanced Border Security and Visa Entry Reform Act with congressional members in attendance, May 2002. The act, along with the USA PATRIOT Act, was passed in response to the September 2001 terrorist attacks.

The Department of Homeland Security, with regards to immigration, is organized as follows: The Bureau of Customs and Border Protection (BCBP) contains Customs and Immigration inspectors, who check the documents of travelers to the United States at air, sea, and land ports of entry; and Border Patrol agents, the uniformed agents who seek to prevent unlawful entry along the southern and northern border. The new Bureau of Immigration and Customs Enforcement (BICE) employs investigators, who attempt to find undocumented immigrants inside the United States, and Detention and Removal officers, who detain and seek to deport such individuals. The new Bureau of Citizenship and Immigration Services (BCIS) is where people go, or correspond with, to become U.S. citizens or obtain permission to work or extend their stay in the United States.

Following the terrorist attacks of September 11, 2001, the Department of Justice adopted several measures that did not require new legislation to be passed by Congress. Some of these measures created controversy and raised concerns about civil liberties. For example, FBI and INS agents detained for months more than 1,000 foreign nationals of Middle Eastern descent and refused to release the names of the individuals. It is alleged that the Department of Justice adopted tactics that discouraged the detainees from obtaining legal assistance. The Department of Justice also began requiring foreign nationals from primarily Muslim nations to be fingerprinted and questioned by immigration officers upon entry or if they have been living in the United States. Those involved in the September 11 attacks were not immigrants—people who become permanent residents with a right to stay in the United States—but holders of temporary visas, primarily visitor or tourist visas.

Immigration to the United States Today

Today, the annual rate of legal immigration is lower than that at earlier periods in U.S. history. For example, from 1901 to 1910 approximately 10.4 immigrants per 1,000 U.S. residents came to the United States. Today, the annual rate is about 3.5 immigrants per 1,000 U.S. residents. While the percentage of foreign-born people in the U.S. population has risen above 11 percent, it remains lower than the 13 percent or higher that prevailed in the country from 1860 to 1930. Still, as has been the case previously in U.S. history, some people argue that even legal immigration should be lowered. These people maintain that immigrants take jobs native-born Americans could fill and that U.S. population growth, which immigration contributes to, harms the environment. In 1996 Congress voted against efforts to reduce legal immigration.

Most immigrants (800,000 to one million annually) enter the United States legally. But over the years the undocumented (illegal) portion of the population has increased to about 2.8 percent of the U.S. population—approximately 8 million people in all.

Today, the legal immigration system in the United States contains many rules, permitting only individuals who fit into certain categories to immigrate—and in many cases only after waiting anywhere from 1 to 10 years or more, depending on the demand in that category. The system, representing a compromise among family, employment, and human rights concerns, has the following elements:

A U.S. citizen may sponsor for immigration a spouse, parent, sibling, or minor or adult child.

A lawful permanent resident (green card holder) may sponsor only a spouse or child.

A foreign national may immigrate if he or she gains an employer sponsor.

An individual who can show that he or she has a "well-founded fear of persecution" may come to the country as a refugee—or be allowed to stay as an asylee (someone who receives asylum).

Beyond these categories, essentially the only other way to immigrate is to apply for and receive one of the "diversity" visas, which are granted annually by lottery to those from "underrepresented" countries.

In 1996 changes to the law prohibited nearly all incoming immigrants from being eligible for federal public benefits, such as welfare, during their first five years in the country. Refugees were mostly excluded from these changes. In addition, families who sponsor relatives must sign an affidavit of support showing they can financially take care of an immigrant who falls on hard times.

A Short History of Canadian Immigration

In the 1800s, immigration into Canada was largely unrestricted. Farmers and artisans from England and Ireland made up a significant portion of 19th-century immigrants. England's Parliament passed laws that facilitated and encouraged the voyage to North America, particularly for the poor.

After the United States barred Chinese railroad workers from settling in the country, Canada encouraged the immigration of Chinese laborers to assist in the building of Canadian railways. Responding to the racial views of the time, the Canadian Parliament began charging a "head tax" for Chinese and South Asian (Indian) immigrants in 1885. The fee of $50—later raised to $500—was well beyond the means of laborers making one or two dollars a day. Later, the government sought additional ways to prohibit Asians from entering the country. For example, it decided to require a "continuous journey," meaning that immigrants to Canada had to travel from their country on a boat that made an uninterrupted passage. For immigrants or asylum seekers from Asia this was nearly impossible.

As the 20th century progressed, concerns about race led to further restrictions on immigration to Canada. These restrictions particularly hurt Jewish and other refugees seeking to flee persecution in Europe. Government statistics indicate that Canada accepted no more than 5,000 Jewish refugees before and during the Holocaust.

After World War II, Canada, like the United States, began accepting thousands of Europeans displaced by the war.

Early Indian Immigrants to Canada

Canada's first Indian immigrants were Sikhs, who arrived in 1904 to the cities of Victoria and Vancouver, located in the western province of British Columbia. They were attracted to the area after hearing tales from returning British Indian soldiers about the region's beauty and high wages. During the early 20th century, more Sikhs settled in British Columbia than anywhere else in Canada or the United States.

The Sikhs worked in logging camps and lumber mills. At that time all Canadians were legally British subjects, and as British citizens, Sikhs had the right to vote. According to Harold Coward, history professor at the University of Victoria, by 1908 about 5,000 Indians had arrived, most of them Sikhs. By that point the area's small white population had felt threatened by the Sikhs' numbers, and anti-immigration sentiment had grown considerably.

In 1908, British Columbia's legislature denied Asian immigrants voting and other rights. The same year Canada implemented the "continuous journey" law, which required South Asians to book passage on a ship traveling without stop from their country of origin. Because no ship line traveled continuously from India to Canada, legal immigration was impossible.

In defiance of the regulation, wealthy Sikh merchant Gurdt Singh Sarhali chartered a Japanese steamer, the *Komagata Maru*, and brought many Indian immigrants along for a journey departing from Hong Kong. When the ship arrived in Vancouver Harbor on May 23, 1914, with 376 Indians onboard, it received a hostile reception. Its passengers remained isolated for two months, while Canadian authorities refused to allow food and water to be brought aboard. Eventually, the passengers were deported, except for those few who had previously established residency in British Columbia.

Essentially cut off from their families, some of Canada's Indians returned to India or moved to the United States. In the 1920s, a few wives and children of those who remained in British Columbia were allowed to join them. The continuous journey regulation remained in effect until 1947, when it was removed along with the voting and other restrictions.

In 1999, Canada issued a postage stamp commemorating Sikh Canadian contributions to the country. It depicted a *khanda*, a double-edged sword representing divine knowledge. Revenue Minister Herb Dhaliwal, the first Indian appointed to a cabinet in a Western democracy, attended the unveiling. Dhaliwal's Sikh grandfather immigrated to Canada in 1906.

Canada's laws were modified to accept these war refugees, as well as Hungarians fleeing Communist authorities after the crushing of the 1956 Hungarian Revolution.

The Immigration Act of 1952 in Canada allowed for a "tap on, tap off" approach to immigration, granting administrative authorities the power to allow more immigrants into the country in good economic times, and fewer in times of recession. The shortcoming of such an approach is that there is little evidence immigrants harm a national economy and much evidence they contribute to economic growth, particularly in the growth of the labor force.

In 1966 the government of Prime Minister Lester Pearson introduced a policy statement stressing how immigrants were key to Canada's economic growth. With Canada's relatively small population base, it became clear that in the absence of newcomers, the country would not be able to grow. The policy was introduced four years after Parliament enacted important legislation that eliminated Canada's own version of racially based national-origin quotas.

In 1967 a new law established a points system that awarded entry to potential immigrants using criteria based primarily on an individual's age, language ability, skills, education, family relationships, and job prospects. The total points needed for entry of an immigrant is set by the Minister of Citizenship and Immigration Canada. The new law also established a category for humanitarian (refugee) entry.

The 1976 Immigration Act refined and expanded the possibility for entry under the points system, particularly for those seeking to sponsor family members. The act also expanded refugee and asylum law to comport with Canada's international obligations. The law established five basic categories for immigration into Canada: 1) family; 2) humanitarian; 3) independents (including skilled workers), who immigrate to Canada on their own; 4) assisted relatives; and 5) business immigrants (including investors, entrepreneurs, and the self-employed).

The new Immigration and Refugee Protection Act, which

took effect June 28, 2002, made a series of modifications to existing Canadian immigration law. The act, and the regulations that followed, toughened rules on those seeking asylum and the process for removing people unlawfully in Canada.

The law modified the points system, adding greater flexibility for skilled immigrants and temporary workers to become permanent residents, and evaluating skilled workers on the weight of their transferable skills as well as those of their specific occupation. The legislation also made it easier for employers to have a labor shortage declared in an industry or sector, which would facilitate the entry of foreign workers in that industry or sector.

On family immigration, the act permitted parents to sponsor dependent children up to the age of 22 (previously 19 was the maximum age at which a child could be sponsored for immigration). The act also allowed partners in common-law arrangements, including same-sex partners, to be considered as family members for the purpose of immigration sponsorship. Along with these liberalizing measures, the act also included provisions to address perceived gaps in immigration-law enforcement.

Indian Immigration to the United States

It is unknown exactly how many Indians entered the United States before 1950 because census records list them as "Others" or "Other Asians." Few immigrants from India came before 1965. With such a long distance between North America and South Asia, the United States was not the most popular destination, particularly for students. Wealthier Indians often studied abroad in England instead.

According to the census reports, from 1948 through 1965, approximately 6,474 Indians immigrated to the United States. In 1960, 391 out of 265,398 immigrants arriving to the country were from India. However, by 1965, there were 10,000 to 20,000 Indian immigrants living in America.

The 1960s brought many changes to the United States. By this point a very prosperous country, the United States broadened its international policy, becoming more involved in world affairs. Antiwar demonstrators protested the prolonged U.S. involvement in Vietnam. President Lyndon B. Johnson signed into law his Great Society social reform bills, which included measures on Medicare and other forms of federal aid. And Congress eliminated racially based admission policies by passing the Immigration Act of 1965.

The new immigration policy also would allow the United States to bring educated, skilled newcomers to its shores. The U.S. space program, military contractors, universities, and aircraft companies hoped to attract scientists and engineers. Great Society medical programs required more doctors. When President Johnson signed the immigration bill in a ceremony at the Statue of Liberty on October 3, 1965, he stated that the new law "says simply that from this day forth those wishing to

In 2001, many U.S. school districts facing teaching shortages went overseas to recruit teachers, a number of whom came from India. Recruiters for public schools in Cleveland, Ohio, specifically targeted Indian teachers.

immigrate to America shall be admitted on the basis of their skills and their close relationship to those already here."

When the new law came into full effect in 1968, it removed barriers to Asian immigration. Also, travel to the United States was within the means of many since airfares were relatively inexpensive. As a result, large extended families of Asians began to arrive. According to INS reports, 27,189 Indians arrived during the 1960s, ready to begin a new life in America.

In the 1970s, American companies such as IBM and Xerox were hiring Indian engineers. Technicians, scientists, doctors, engineers, and scholars came as well. By 1980, Indian Americans numbered almost 400,000. Another quarter-million came during the 1980s. By 1990, there were more than 450,000 Indian immigrants living in the United States and more than 800,000 of Indian descent.

The 1990s hi-tech boom generated thousands of computer-related jobs that went unfilled. An estimated 1.6 million high-tech jobs were available in 2000. At the time, India was graduating 73,000 information technology professionals each year from 6 institutes of technology and 43 private and regional colleges. In the United States, some of these graduates were offered positions paying as much as 10 times what they would earn in India. Also, many Indians were hired by U.S. firms after completing graduate degrees at American universities.

From 1990 to 2000, the Indian immigrant population in the United States rose 124 percent, from 450,000 to 1 million, a higher increase than that of any other Asian country. By 1999, India ranked fourth as a source country of immigration behind Mexico, the Philippines, and China.

It is difficult to overstate the important and positive impact that Indian-born professionals have had on American technology and job creation. According to AnnaLee Saxenian, a University of California associate professor, in 2000 Indian and Chinese entrepreneurs managed 29 percent of Silicon Valley's technology businesses. These companies combined to account for $19.5 billion in sales and 72,839 jobs in that year. Vinod

4 Making a New Life

Indian immigrants to North America make many sacrifices. They leave a home where they knew most or all of their neighbors and arrive in a place where they may know no one at all. Middle-class immigrants may give up having servants to do their cooking, cleaning, and gardening, and their new jobs may mean lower status even though they may receive higher pay. Some immigrants who have advanced degrees but lack Canadian or American professional licenses must first accept menial jobs. Like all immigrants, the dream of a better life for them and their families remains their inspiration during difficult times.

Settling In

Most immigrants are motivated to work hard and succeed. They are adventurous enough to strike out on their own to a place hundreds—or even thousands—of miles from home. Often their strong sense of family and community helps them succeed. Relatives may lend them money to buy or start a business. Older relatives in the household may help with housework and childcare, freeing up parents to work long hours. Immigrants who have built successful businesses may hire new arrivals from their country.

When immigrants arrive to the United States, they are often surprised to find that life is not like what they have seen in Hollywood movies. Some are surprised by the cultural diversity

◀A Sikh American taxi driver sits behind the wheel of his vehicle. Taxi driving is one of the many trades that Indian Americans have entered in the United States. In New York City, an estimated 70 percent of the cab drivers hail from India, Pakistan, or Bangladesh.

or by the fact that most people live in ordinary homes instead of mansions. Customs and slang may confuse even the well educated.

Most Indian arrivals at least have the advantage of speaking English and having some familiarity with Western-style institutions. But even when a job is waiting for them, they must first find housing and transportation and open a bank account. Some employers arrange temporary housing and transportation for foreign employees, or they pair the new hire with a mentor. Family members who are already settled may also help immigrants get started in their new lives.

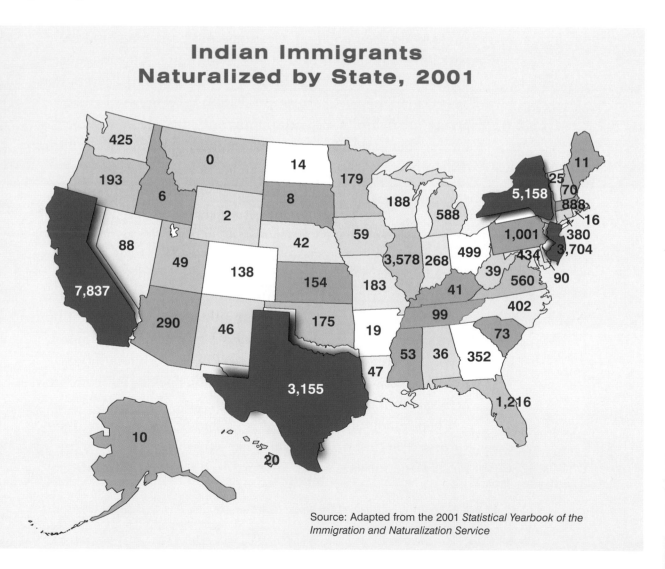

Indian Immigrants Naturalized by State, 2001

Source: Adapted from the 2001 *Statistical Yearbook of the Immigration and Naturalization Service*

Immigrant parents hope for a better education and more opportunities for their children than they had. They expect their children to excel in school, and usually they do excel. A report of the Children of Immigrants Longitudinal Study, conducted in Southern California between 1992 and 1996, found that second-generation Indian high school students ranked second only to Chinese students among immigrant groups in terms of high grade averages and low dropout rates.

Indians settle in big cities, suburbs, and small towns, often near universities, hospitals, or high-tech corporations. The highest concentrations of Indian Americans live in California, New York, New Jersey, Texas, and Illinois. There are more than 300,000 Indian Americans in California, over 200,000 in New York State, and over 100,000 in New Jersey, Texas, and Illinois.

Many Indian immigrants have settled in the metropolitan areas of New York; San Francisco, California; Miami, Florida; and Chicago, Illinois. Other thriving Indian communities exist in Tampa Bay, Florida; Seattle, Washington; Los Angeles and the San Jose–Palo Alto region (Silicon Valley), California; and Detroit, Michigan.

Indian Settlement in Major U.S. Cities

Traditionally a gateway for newly arrived foreigners, New York City has drawn more immigrants than any other American city. Many Indian Americans living in New York City hail from the cities of Mumbai and Gujarat. Newcomers and first- and second-generation immigrants alike enjoy the proximity of Indian restaurants and groceries, mosques, and Hindu temples. Indian immigrants have established a niche in some job fields, paving the way for other newcomers. A popular job among Indians living in New York is driving taxis: the Taxi and Limousine Commission of New York City estimated that about 70 percent of the city's cab drivers are immigrants from India, Pakistan, and Bangladesh.

The greater metropolitan area of New York also attracts

Indian immigrants. From 1990 to 1995, a large number of Indian newcomers settled in the borough of Queens, mostly in the Jackson Heights neighborhood. There merchants established a "Little India" shopping area and organized to deal with civic issues. Today some Indian Americans are moving farther beyond the city. The Indian American population in Westchester County grew significantly between 1980 and 2000.

An estimated 150,000 Indian Americans, many from Gujarat, live in northern California. The San Francisco Bay Area Federation of Indo-American Associations organizes events such as an Independence Day celebration, complete with parades, concerts, and visiting Bollywood film stars. At Thanksgiving, Bay Area Indian Americans feed San Jose's homeless and distribute winter blankets.

Over the years, Northside Chicago and its nearby suburbs drew many Indian doctors, engineers, and scientists, who later sponsored their relatives. The 1990 U.S. Census reported that

Indian restaurants line the streets of the Little India section of New York's Greenwich Village. Another Little India has sprung up in the Queens borough of New York, and similar neighborhoods are found in major cities like Toronto, San Fransisco, and Miami.

Chicago's Indian American community grew from 31,858 to 57,992 over the previous decade. By the 1990s, most new arrivals were university students and computer professionals. The Chicago area today is home to some 350,000 Indian Americans.

In the years following World War II, a Chicago neighborhood along Devon Avenue, originally named by English settlers for Devonshire England, became a Jewish community shopping

Helping Two Communities

Known around Tampa, Florida, as "Dr. K," cardiologist Kiran C. Patel has given back much to his native and adopted countries. Patel was born in the African country of Zambia but grew up in Gujarat, India. His father, an accountant, pushed him hard in his academic studies. "My father said that if I were second in my class, I should not even bother to put my foot in the house," Patel told the *Tampa Tribune*.

After graduating from Cambridge University and the University of London in England, Patel completed his medical degree at Gujarat University in 1974. He moved to the United States in 1976 after completing residencies in India and Zambia. Patel received additional medical training at Jersey City Medical Center before accepting a fellowship at Columbia University in New York City.

In 1982 Patel started his practice in Tampa. Two years later, with one employee, he founded a physician practice management company. In 1992, he bought Well Care, a small HMO, which he eventually built up into Florida's largest Medicaid provider—a $1-billion business employing 1,200. In July 2002, he sold Well Care to New York investors for an undisclosed sum.

Dr. K and his wife, pediatrician Dr. Pallavi Patel, have shared a great deal of their accumulated wealth. They were instrumental in establishing the India Cultural Center in Tampa, and started a college scholarship fund for underprivileged students. They also helped fund the construction of a modern 50-bed hospital and school in Gujarat. In October 2002, Dr. Patel donated $5 million to the Tampa Bay Performing Arts Center. Chairman of Visionary Medical Systems, a medical software company, Dr. Patel also has served as president of the American Association of Physicians of Indian Origin.

center. In the 1970s, Indian immigrants began to establish businesses in that neighborhood, opening grocery stores, restaurants, video and gift shops, and stores offering jewelry and saris (a traditional dress worn by Indian women). Ultimately the neighborhood became known as Indiatown, recognized as a major marketplace of Indian goods and services.

During the 1980s, an economic recession increased the need for social services in Chicago. Nearly 18 percent of the city's Indian population was reported to live below the poverty level. In order to provide health and family services for Chicago's Indian population, activists founded the nonprofit Indo-American Center in 1996, and set up the organization's headquarters in the former Jewish Community Center building. At the center immigrants can take literacy and civics classes, as well as receive help filling out application forms to become U.S. citizens. Chicago-area temples and mosques take part in feeding the homeless and other charitable activities.

Southern and Midwestern Communities

The 2000 U.S. Census reported that Georgia's Indian community increased 231 percent over the previous decade, and that Indians had become the state's largest Asian group. As of 2000, there were 46,000 Indian Americans residing in Georgia. Initially, many Indian graduate students came to the area to attend the universities; immigrants arriving later came for high-tech jobs located in Atlanta and other cities. Indian Festivals at Atlanta's Civic Center feature pageants, folk music and dances, seminars, workshops, food, and arts and crafts.

In 2001, Florida's Tampa Bay area was home to an estimated 3,500 Indian American families, many from Gujarat. Some 550 families belong to the Gujarati Samaj of Tampa Bay Association. The group first sponsored small, informal Gujarati festival celebrations that were held during the 1970s and 1980s. Using recorded music and makeshift costumes, women danced the *garba*, a circular, whirling folk dance. As more events were

In Atlanta, Georgia, the Indian community has been thriving since the 1990s. Between 1990 and 2000 the Indian population of the state grew 231 percent; a large segment of this group was comprised of university students specializing in various high-tech fields.

held and membership grew, the organization took on greater projects. In 1996, it completed the India Cultural Center. The group sponsors *garba* competitions and other events, including an annual India Festival.

A group of Indians, mainly composed of university students, began migrating to Cleveland, Ohio, as early as the 1920s. According to census reports, the community grew from 100 in the 1930s to 5,780 in 1990. Most of the immigrants came from Gujarat. Later arrivals included a greater number of doctors, engineers, and other professionals. The newcomers first settled close to hospitals and colleges on the city's east side. In the 1970s immigrants and first- and second-generation Indians began settling farther away from the city in the western suburbs.

In December 1962, when India was in the midst of a five-year-old border conflict with China, a small assembly of 100 people attended a meeting in Cleveland to discuss the recent Chinese invasion of India. By 1964 that group had evolved into the India Association of Cleveland. The creation of other organizations followed, including the India Community Center. Established in 1976, the center offered courses in Indian cooking, languages, dance, and music. The center also showed documentaries about India, operated a speaker's bureau, and published *The Lotus*, a free monthly newspaper for the Indian community.

Many of the Indians who arrived to St. Louis in the mid-1960s were college and medical students. Many of these students stayed after completing their degrees, helping establish an Indian community that continued to thrive during the 1990s, when the local information technology industry provided numerous jobs. Indians and Indian Americans were employed as doctors, chemists, scientists, programmers, and professors. Those who owned businesses ran liquor stores, markets, and Indian restaurants.

The Indian community of St. Louis, reported to number 4,000 people in 1999, continues to thrive today. Some companies specialize in meeting the particular needs of the community: Seema Enterprises and Shriji Enterprises run travel agencies and stores that sell Indian foods, CDs, books, and movies. The Mahatma Gandhi Center, next door to the Hindu temple, offers cultural programs such as demonstrations by traditional dance troupes. In 1997, the India Association of St. Louis sponsored a festival celebrating the 50th anniversary of India's independence from Great Britain.

After the oil boom ended in 1982, the city of Houston, Texas, neared financial collapse. The city, which had depended heavily on the oil industry, no longer attracted young professionals, and many longtime residents moved away as the job market steadily declined over the next five years. As Houston recovered, reinvented itself, diversified, and grew, its leaders focused on bringing in new industries. Community leaders considered immigration vital to the city's economic health, so they campaigned to an international audience, aiming to generate positive attitudes about Houston.

In 1995, 984 Indian Americans lived in Houston, and their

numbers were reported to still be growing in the early years of the 21st century. Several local organizations serving the growing Indian American population have been established, including the city's Indo-America Charity Foundation and the Indo-American Association, which promotes the cultural arts. In 2001, local business people founded the Indo-American Chamber of Commerce of Greater Houston. Comprised of 150 members, the organization offers mentoring services to other business people and provides them with networking opportunities.

Indian Communities in Canada

In Canada, most Indians settle in the three largest cities—Toronto, Vancouver, and Montreal. Clifford Kraus reported in

The city of Vancouver, British Columbia, is home to Canada's second-largest Indian community, of which Sikh Indians make up a large segment. The first Sikh school established in North America is in Vancouver.

Indian professionals to found organizations that championed more service-oriented goals. The groups met to discuss issues of common interest or help with development projects in India.

In the late summer of 1989, more than 3,000 Indian expatriates met in New York City to discuss common concerns and problems. As a result, the Global Organization of People of Indian Origin formed, with the goal to promote interests, cultural heritage, and interaction between Indian communities. Among the activities offered were workshops for entrepreneurs.

One of the largest Indian professional groups is the American Association of Physicians of Indian Origin. It claims a membership of 35,000 physicians and 10,000 medical students and residents.

In the hospitality industry, a popular field of investment for Indian entrepreneurs, Indians have formed advocacy groups to combat discrimination. In 1985, Midsouth Indemnity Association, which later became the National Indo-American Hospitality Association, formed in Tennessee. The Asian American Hotel Owners Association formed in Atlanta in 1989. In 1994 the two groups merged to become the Atlanta-based Asian American Hotel Owners Association.

Membership in the Asian American Hotel Owners Association grew from fewer than 300 in 1989 to more than 6,000 by 2002. Its members today own more than 17,000 hotels valued at almost $40 billion, and employ almost 800,000 people. Collectively, the hotels comprise more than half of the economy hotels, and more than a third of the total hotels in America.

Perhaps the most well-known Indian professional group, IndUS Entrepreneurs, was established in 1992 to help new immigrants overcome obstacles. The founding members, high-tech executives and businesspeople from India and neighboring countries, provided mentoring, advice to streamline ideas, and free legal and accounting services. Members back startup companies and help them find skilled tech workers. Monthly meetings feature expert speakers and networking opportunities.

IndUS Entrepreneurs operates ten chapters in the United States and five in India. More than 400 members belong to the Southern California chapter.

In addition to the scores of professional organizations, groups have also formed to serve the religious and cultural interests of Indian immigrants. Members of these groups hope to pass their heritage and history to future generations. Hundreds of these local groups, many specialized according to religion, region, or language, operate throughout North America.

5 KEEPING THE CULTURE ALIVE

Just as a new student in school wants to feel comfortable, make friends, and succeed, a foreigner in a new country wants to build a life and become comfortable in that new environment. He or she may choose to dress and act like the native people while at the same time aiming to preserve the culture and heritage of the homeland.

People have a multitude of different ideas about what it means to be American, Canadian, Indian, or a mixture of these nationalities. Indians living in North America typically distinguish among themselves those who are American- or Canadian-born, or at least longtime residents, and those who are newly arrived, are not yet English-speaking, and wear native dress. Assimilation is the process by which an immigrant becomes part of mainstream society. Using slang or wearing Western fashions are just a few examples of assimilation.

The Faiths of Indian Immigrants

Indian immigrants who came to North America before the 1960s tried to fit in more than stand out, an approach that was not always easy in countries where few women wore saris or *bindis*. Today most Indian immigrants carry on their country's heritage by following the religion they practiced in India. Among these various faiths are Hinduism, Islam, Jainism, Parsism, and Sikhism.

◀ An Indian Sikh market owner, wearing a turban as a symbol of his faith, displays his merchandise in Vancouver, Canada. Many immigrants practicing the various religions of the homeland strive to maintain their customs and tenets.

Part of Indian culture for 5,000 years, Hinduism is one of the world's oldest religions. Owing to the multitude of Hindu sects, specific beliefs vary throughout India. Much of the religion is preserved through dedication to rituals and ceremony. Most Hindus accept the caste system and consider the Vedas the most sacred of the ancient scriptures. Hindus also believe that Karma, a force of destiny, propels living beings through a cycle of birth and rebirth. All Hindu gods, such as Rama, Krishna, Shiva, and the elephant-headed god Ganesha, are considered forms of one Supreme Being.

The earliest Hindu immigrants prayed in makeshift facilities ranging from mattress showrooms to YMCA buildings. After the establishment of the Hindu Temple Society of North America in 1970, the organization built one of North America's first Hindu temples in Flushing, New York. While Hindu temples in India are open shrines designed for individual prayer, North American temples are constructed to accommodate group worship. To suit working schedules, temples hold events on Sundays, which is not done in India. Just as classical Indian dancers might perform at a Catholic mass in India, American Hindu worship often exhibits an American influence.

A Hindu monk wears the mask of Shiva, one of many Hindu gods believed to be part of the one Supreme Being. Hindu temples have been built in North America, although many differ in design from those in India.

Islam is the second most popular faith among Indian immigrants. The word *Islam* comes from the Arabic verb *aslama*, which roughly means "to gain peace by submitting to the will of God." The religion is based on the teachings of Muhammad, born in Mecca in 570. His revelations concerning the oneness of God, Allah, and the folly of worshipping idols are written in the Qur'an, the sacred text of Islam. Islam defines a distinct way of behavior for a universal community worshipping one God. In contrast, Hinduism is also a distinct way of life, yet recognizes many gods and asserts inequalities between people. Many Muslims in India follow a doctrine that has been long integrated into Indian culture.

One of the first meeting places in North America for Muslims was the Islamic Center in Michigan City, Indiana, built in the early 1900s. For many years most Muslims lacked access to mosques and met for worship in rented halls or cafes. Today, there are temples and mosques throughout Canada and the United States.

Jainism originated in India, where Jains make up class of wealthy professionals. They are followers of Mahavira, a prince in northeast India who reigned during the fifth century B.C. Appalled by the region's poverty, Mahavira sought to reform the Hindu caste system that helped create the poor conditions of his people.

Jains believe in reincarnation, nonviolence, and respect for the environment. They practice meditation and self-denial, believing that desire causes suffering and that the good life is attained only through deprivation. As strict vegetarians, their reverence for life runs so deep they avoid even accidentally stepping on an insect. They respect other viewpoints and live by the "Three Jewels" of right conduct, right knowledge, and right worldview.

To preserve their religion against the spread of Islam, the Parsis from ancient Persia fled Iran more than 1,000 years ago. The king of Gujarat offered them refuge, and they lived peacefully with the Hindus. Followers of the Iranian prophet

Zoroaster, they adhere to the three virtues of "good thoughts, good words, good deeds." Fairer skinned and taller than most Indians, they are the most Westernized of India's ethnic groups.

Based mainly in Mumbai, the Parsis are mainly middle class and well educated. Originally farmers and artisans, under British rule the Parsis built most of India's industry and amassed fortunes. Some changed their last names to fit their occupations, frequently tacking on the suffix *-wala*, meaning "dealer" or "manufacturer." This resulted in intriguing Parsi surnames such as Printer, Readymoney, and Sodabottleopenerwala.

A Sikh delegation presents a holy sword to Congress Party leader Sonia Gandhi as part of the celebration of Gurupurab, which recognizes the birth anniversary of Guru Nanak, founder of the Sikh faith. Gurupurab remains a popular celebration among Sikhs in North America.

The Hare Krishna Movement

An offshoot of Hinduism, the New York City–based Hare Krishna movement attracted many young followers during the 1960s. Sporting shaved heads and saffron color robes, they danced, chanted, beat drums, and jingled bells on the streets, asking for change. A. C. Bhaktivedanta Swami Prabhupada founded the movement in Calcutta in 1896 and brought it to New York in 1965.

Hare Krishnas follow the holy book Bhagavad-Gita and believe the Hindu god Krishna took human form to save mankind from a materialistic existence. The International Society for Krishna Consciousness was founded in Great Britain in 1968, and George Harrison of the rock band the Beatles became its most famous devotee. Hare Krishna's Food for Life Program operates free restaurants, homeless shelters, and provides emergency relief in 60 countries.

George Harrison (left) sits with members of the Hare Krishna sect, 1969.

The Sikh religion was founded in the 15th century in Punjab, a lush northwestern agricultural region. It is founded primarily on the teachings of 10 gurus. The first guru, Nanak, was enlightened by God's message after he disappeared for three days in the Bain River. Three hundred years after Nanak was first enlightened, the 10th guru, Gobind Singh, declared the principles of the faith: sacrifice, chastity, courage, service, and struggle against injustice. Sikh followers are required to wear certain symbols of faith, including a turban, dagger, combs, and bracelets. They reject the caste system and consider it their duty to help make the world a better place.

Although Buddhism originated in India, only a small group of Buddhists, mainly refugees from China and converted lower

caste Hindus, lives there today. Founded in 525 B.C. by Siddhartha Gautama—the Buddha—Buddhism thrived throughout India until the 13th century. A revival of Hinduism and invasions by Huns and Muslims contributed to its decline. Buddhists believe in reincarnation, or a cycle of birth and rebirth. They stress the importance of meditation and follow basic moral rules.

Traditional attire for Indian women includes a sari and a *dupatta* (a scarf draped over the shoulder). A more complete outfit will add a jacket and *salwar* (pants).

Traditional Clothing and Food

Most Indian women in North America wear Western clothing except on special occasions. Today's Indian designers create both traditional styles and Westernized modern designs. A sari is worn with a *dupatta* (a scarf draped over the shoulder), and a *lehanga* is a jacket, flared skirt, and dupatta. A *salwar lehanga* combines the jacket, skirt, and *dupatta* with *salwar* (pants). Many Indian women wear a pantsuit known as a *churidaar*. The pants are tight at the bottom with fabric draped over the ankles to resemble bangles. A top called a *kameez* is worn over the pants and is worn with a dupatta.

Up until the end of the 1960s, there were few Indian stores in North America, so immigrants would ask their relatives to purchase saris and traditional jewelry when they visited India. In return, they supplied Western items to relatives living in India.

During the period when there was a lack of Indian restaurants and Indian grocery stores, even in the major cities, Indian immigrants struggled to maintain a similar diet to what they had in their homeland. The central problem was that many Indians are vegetarian, and there were few shopping opportunities for them. The vegetarian practice originated in India, where many people seriously follow the religious ethic of being in harmony with creation. Three of the country's major religions—Hinduism, Jainism, and Buddhism—believe in *ashimsa* (nonviolence), a principle that applies to the treatment of all living things, including animals. However, some Indians who were vegetarian in their native countries began eating meat after emigrating.

Before the 1970s, mainstream restaurants did not offer vegetarian menu selections. Indian cooking ingredients were not available, so some immigrants improvised with what was available to them. Relatives also mailed spices from India, or immigrants brought them back from a visit to the country. Makeshift homemade Indian cuisine was often served at weekend social gatherings.

Enterprising immigrants decided to meet the needs of their community. In 1970, Gorthandas Soni and his brother opened House of Spices in Flushing, New York, and began to provide high-quality imported Indian food. Today the company operates retail stores throughout the United States, selling grains, specialty rice, spices, pickles, chutney, and Indian sweets and snacks. It also manufactures its own food products.

In the 21st century, Indians can obtain almost any food they would find in India, thanks in part to a growing interest in vegetarianism and the popularity of Indian cuisine. Vegetarian offerings include salad bars, soybean meat imitations, veggie

Following a Dream

Rachna Gilmore grew up in an upper-middle-class family who lived in a Georgian mansion in Mumbai. When she was young girl, she first heard of her future home country, Canada, listening to her fourth-grade teacher read the novel *Anne of Green Gables* to the class.

Originally planning to study medicine, Gilmore received a bachelor's of science in 1974 from King's College in London. Afterward, she decided to travel, ultimately moving to Prince Edward Island, Canada, where she married and earned a bachelor's degree in elementary education.

In Canada, Gilmore worked as a paralegal researcher, then set up a pottery studio in her basement. After her two daughters were born in 1980 and 1984, the family moved to Ottawa. There, at age 30, Gilmore began to pursue her dream of writing.

Her first picture book, *My Mother is Weird*, was published in 1986. Her second children's book, *Wheniwasalittlegirl*, followed close behind. Under the pseudonym Rachna Mara, she published an adult short story collection entitled *Of Custom and Excise* in 1991. Gleaning material from her Indian background, she wrote *Lights for Gita*, the first in a Gita series that also includes *Roses for Gita* and *A Gift for Gita*. Her young-adult novel, *A Group of One*, written with a grant from the Department of Canadian Heritage, tells the story of a grandmother from India who visits her Westernized immigrant family in Ottawa.

burgers and pizzas, vegetarian restaurants, and meatless pet foods. Taj brand frozen entrées include 12 varieties of Indian vegetarian dinners with organic rice and vegetables. Gourmet ethnic foods can also be ordered off the Internet.

Preserving Indian Heritage

Many recent immigrants consider themselves Americans or Canadians who are keeping alive their Indian culture. They use dance performances, music, literature, movies, art exhibitions, cultural workshops, religious rituals, and festivals to preserve their Indian heritage. For example, in 1996 an organization called the Asian Indian Historical Archive Committee recorded the experiences and perspectives of 12 of its members by producing a video documentary that filmed daily life in their Ohio homes.

First- and second-generation Indian writers have recorded their experiences through acclaimed poetry and fiction. In 1977, American-born novelist Clark Blaise and his wife, novelist Bharati Mukherjee, published a joint autobiographical account of their year in her native India called *Days and Nights in Calcutta*. G. S. Sharat Chandra's 1998 short story collection, *Sari of the Gods*, deals with Indian immigrants in North America.

Two young girls light candles and oil lamps for the Hindu celebration of Diwali (Festival of Lights). Many immigrants return to India for the festival, which celebrates the New Year and the victory of good over evil.

Festivals, Parades, and Dance Performances

Diwali, the Festival of Lights, triggers a deep nostalgia for most Indians. Originally an ancient harvest celebration, it was later incorporated into the Hindu calendar of holidays and became a celebration of the new year. The holiday occurs in the Hindu month of Ashvin, which falls in October or November. Diwali celebrates the triumph of good over evil, commemorating Lord Rama's return to his birthplace after slaying Ravana, a 10-headed demon king. Diwali also marks the victory of Krishna, the celestial cowherd, over the demon Narakasura.

The events of Diwali begin 10 days or more in advance. The home is cleaned and decorated. Abstract *rangoli* designs made of natural materials such as rice, flower petals, or tinted rice flour adorn the entrance. They are then destroyed the first time a person walks through the door. Special foods are prepared, and Indians wear new clothes and exchange multicolor sweets with friends, neighbors, and business associates. During Diwali season, the House of Spices' Shamiana candy division works around the clock to produce 2,000 to 3,000 pounds of Indian sweets per day.

Shruti Sharma represented India as a contestant in the Miss World 2002 competition. The Indian community in North America holds its own contests, called the "Miss India U.S." and "Miss India Canada" pageants, in which contestants are judged on their performance of Indian folk and classical dances.

In India, Hindus observe Diwali by lighting thousands of clay oil lamps and candles and setting them on balconies and window ledges. They are placed there to welcome and light the way for Laksmi, the Hindu goddess of wealth, and Genesh, the god of good fortune and wisdom. Street musicians play and firecrackers, cherry bombs, and bottle rockets explode everywhere. The lighting of roman candles is a way to express joy, and is also believed to scare away evil spirits.

Many immigrants may take their children to visit India during the Diwali celebrations, or they may try to re-create them for their children, though in an entirely different form. Because it is a public holiday in India, Diwali may fall on a workday in North America, and in some communities fireworks are banned. In her book *Lights for Gita*, author Rachna Gilmore tells the story of an immigrant family celebrating Diwali in America for the first time. The title character experiences a quiet celebration on a dark wintry night, in contrast to the excitement of New Delhi's public festival ablaze with fireworks, celebrated in the company of extended family.

In some Indian American communities, Diwali celebrations are nearly as elaborate as those in India. Festivities include street fairs, balls, luncheons, parades, dance parties, and fireworks displays. Along Chicago's Devon Avenue, colored lights from the Diwali festival are sometimes mistaken for Christmas decorations. The San Francisco Bay area's first Diwali Mela in 1994 combined festivities with fund-raising for a temple. Hundreds of lights sparkle along Jackson Heights' 74th Street in New York for the annual Diwali street fair, attended by more than 10,000 people.

Another significant holiday for Indians worldwide is celebrated on August 15, the date that India gained its independence from British colonial rule in 1947. Many North American cities hold Independence Day parades. In Chicago, the local Federation of Indian Associations and large corporations sponsor the event. Indian movie stars, beauty queens, and political figures serve as the grand marshal and guests of honor.

In October or November, the Hindu festival Navaratri Mahotsav, or "Festival of Nine Nights," recognize another victory of good over evil. According to legend, the goddess Durga appeared to kill an evil spirit that could not be slain by any male. Especially popular in western India, Navratri celebrations vary from region to region. In Gujarat, a giant statue symbolizing evil is burned on the 10th day of the celebration. In North America, local universities and Indian associations sponsor Navratri festivals.

Other local festivals promote Indian culture. The India Association of Long Island organizes New York's Indiafest, which features Indian foods and stalls selling traditional clothing and Indian CDs. Local dance troupes perform traditional dances.

All Indian dance genres stem from the 2,000-year-old Natya Shastras (Theatre Scriptures) that portray scenes from Hindu mythology. The various Indian classical dance forms require years of practice and discipline. Most dancers specialize in one form. The performances of many Indian folk dances have become competitive events. *Bhangra*, a Punjabi folk dance and musical style, has become so popular that George Washington University, in Washington, D.C., sponsors an annual intercollegiate competition called the Bhangra Blowout. The Federation of Gujarati Association in North America organizes the North American Raas, a *garba* and folk-dance competition held in Newark, New Jersey. Miss India Worldwide organizes "Miss India U.S." and "Miss India Canada" beauty pageants in which contestants, mainly second-generation Indians, perform classical and folk dances.

Indian music has also found many Western listeners. The late 1980s brought a revival of ancient traditional Gandharva Veda melodies, which are believed to generate tranquility and energy. The "new Bhangra beat" features Indopop performers such as Bally Saghoo, Nitin Sawhney, and Cornershop.

A poster for *Mother India* (1957), a film that launched India's lucrative movie industry, known as Bollywood. By subscribing to satellite television channels and going to special movie theaters, Indian immigrants are able to catch the latest Bollywood releases.

Links Back Home

Some immigrants acknowledge the importance of connections with the homeland and make periodic visits to extended family members in India. Even by plane, the trip is long and expensive. For most Indian immigrants, it is difficult to visit frequently.

Those who cannot make the trip explore the various ways to stay in touch. For the early waves of immigrants, calls back home were expensive, requiring operators and often resulting in poor connections. Calls had to be coordinated to compensate for the 9- to 12-hour time difference between North America and India. Now Indian immigrants can connect with family and friends using less-expensive faxes and e-mails. Internet sites host cyber communities with news and chat rooms for dispersed Indians. Most Indian organizations have websites for members and other people to stay connected.

Owing to the international success of Bollywood, India's thriving film industry, immigrants can keep track of the most recent movie sensations. Bollywood grew from the success of a three-hour epic called *Mother India*, first shown in 1957. Indian cinema has since gained worldwide popularity, though the early immigrants seldom had the opportunity to see Indian films. Today, immigrants can remain up-to-date on all the latest movies and music produced in India. Satellite television stations broadcast Indian TV shows and movies. Some movie theaters show nothing but Indian movies, while video and CD shops sell recordings of movies and Hindi songs from soundtracks.

Changing Generations

First-generation Indian immigrants face many tasks to establish their new lives. They must deal with obtaining legal status, settling into a home, and achieving financial security. Many keep their own company and seldom venture out of the immediate community. Some feel that they are too busy to maintain their religious traditions.

The second generation—the children of Indian immigrants—may share their parents' values but from a different viewpoint. Frequently, they feel more comfortable in Western society and are accustomed to enjoying more freedoms. Like many young people, the children of Indian immigrants see their parents as too conservative. In turn, their parents worry that their sons and daughters will become too materialistic or too Westernized and lose their religious identity and culture.

The children of Indian immigrants may clash with their parents over permission to participate in activities unfamiliar to them, such as coed parties or proms. Many parents allow their children to eventually find their own partners rather than arrange marriages for them, but they maintain hope that their sons and daughters will marry within their own culture.

As settled as Indian immigrants may become in their new country, many never stop yearning for their first home. Author Jhumpa Lahiri, a second-generation immigrant, said in a 1999 *Newsweek International* interview, "I've inherited my parents' preoccupations. It's hard to have parents who consider another place 'home'—even after living abroad for 30 years, India is home for them."

Returning Home

Some Indian immigrants arrive in the United States or Canada expecting to stay just long enough to save a satisfactory amount of money for a comfortable retirement and then return home. However, not all who plan to return do so. After living many years abroad, they lose the connection with their homeland or the decision to return becomes impractical.

When the Internet was launched in India in 1996, many enterprising computer professionals were presented with new opportunities. Some who had been working in North America raised enough money to start up technology companies in India. The lower wages they could pay programmers in India enabled these entrepreneurs to operate their businesses at reduced costs.

Only about 1,500 Indians working in high-technology jobs in the United States returned home in 1999, less than 1/30 of the number arriving, according to an August 2000 report in *The Industry Standard*. However, since the American economy weakened after that time, it is likely that subsequent downsizing of businesses will increase the number of Indians returning home.

6 HUMAN SMUGGLING AND WORKER EXPLOITATION

Undocumented Indian immigrants can face many serious problems in North America. If they are discovered, they face prosecution by immigration authorities; if they remain undiscovered, they are in danger of being exploited, especially by employers in search of cheap labor.

Undocumented immigrants either sneak across a border or enter a country legally but overstay their visas. They may use phony identity documents, make false asylum claims and then disappear while awaiting a hearing, or carry out marriage, family relation, or work visa fraud. It is unknown exactly how many undocumented immigrants reside in North America; analysts estimated that in 2000 there were approximately 8.5 million living in the United States. A number of estimates have concluded that in the New York metropolitan area there are over 500,000 undocumented residents, many of whom hail from Pakistan, Iraq, Turkey, and India.

Human Smuggling

The United States made a more focused effort to tighten its borders against illegal immigration after a rusty freighter named the *Golden Venture* ran aground in 1993 off New York's Rockaway Peninsula. Aboard the vessel were 286 Chinese immigrants, who had each paid smugglers $35,000 for passage to America. When the ship became caught on the rocks, the smugglers released the passengers into 53-degree

◀ A man apprehended after trying to illegally immigrate sits alone in a holding cell. The road from India to North America is a dangerous one for undocumented immigrants, and many of those who arrive safely still face the danger of being exploited in the workplace.

ocean waters; 10 passengers died while trying to swim to shore. The police and Coast Guard rescued the others.

Federal officials can wiretap phone conversations to track down illegal operations, but smugglers have avoided detection by using beepers, cell phones, and telephone calling cards. During the 1990s the thriving economy of the United States attracted large numbers of undocumented immigrants. The majority of undocumented immigrants are Mexicans, but many also come from Asian countries, including India. According to a 2003 report by the former INS Office of Policy and Planning, which used data from the 2000 census report, an estimated 70,000 undocumented Indians reside in the United States.

A federal undercover investigation undertaken in 1994 turned up hundreds of undocumented Indian and Pakistani immigrants in New York City. Through smugglers, the immigrants had arranged to buy fake employment and entry documents—costing between $500 and $2,000—from INS agents posing as corrupt officials. When the undocumented immigrants arrived at a warehouse to pick up their documents, the smugglers were arrested and the immigrants served with deportation notices.

In 1997, the INS dismantled a smuggling gang that was transporting about 50 undocumented immigrants, mostly from India and Pakistan, to Houston and other cities each month. The gang would receive $28,000 for each immigrant smuggled. Recruited by the smugglers in India and Pakistan, the immigrants were flown to Moscow, Russia, where it was easy to arrange flights and obtain travel papers. They then flew to Managua, Nicaragua, and from there they were driven in vans or trucks to a safe house located just south of the Texas or Arizona border. Later, guides led them across the border into the United States.

In March 1998, federal officials broke up a smuggling ring that over a seven-month period brought approximately 1,000 undocumented immigrants from India, China, and Nepal into the United States, at a charge of as much as $30,000 per individual. A yearlong federal investigation ending in November

1998 disbanded the largest immigrant smuggling cartel in U.S. history. Thirty-one people were indicted for immigration violations and money laundering. Over a three-year period, the ring brought in 300 immigrants per month, approximately 12,000 overall, mostly single men from India. The immigrant or a prospective employer paid the smugglers' fees of $20,000 to $28,000 per individual, enabling the cartel to gross about $220 million.

In the spring of 2001, the Canadian Council of Professional Engineers (CCPE) alerted immigration officials to a scam involving illegal immigration into Canada. Immigrants from India and China claiming to be engineers were entering the country using phony transcripts and resumes, then disappearing once inside the country. The CCPE had become suspicious after reviewing the false documents of a number of the immigrants.

Worker Exploitation

Actually making it to the United States or Canada does not ensure success for undocumented immigrants, as they can be taken advantage of after reaching their destination. Smugglers have been known to seize the newcomers' passports or other documents. Undocumented immigrants have been forced by threats or physical abuse to work long hours in barricaded sweatshops for pay far below minimum wage.

Often undocumented immigrants are afraid to quit their jobs because they don't know anyone in the country, don't understand the language, and have little or no money. They are reluctant to report dangerous working conditions. Uninformed about the U.S. civil rights and labor laws that protect undocumented immigrants, they seldom contact authorities for help, fearful of being deported. Smugglers or employers may set up arrangements in which workers agree to work to pay off a debt, but the employers may rig the contracts so that they never end. For instance, an employer might add on to an immigrant's debt by accusing him or her of ruining property.

Government crackdowns on smugglers protect undocumented

workers and shut down shops run by corrupt employers. In the past, INS investigators worked to uphold the 1986 federal law imposing civil and criminal penalties on employers who knowingly hired undocumented immigrants. The immigrants would be detained, then deported and subsequently barred from reentering the United States for up to 10 years. These responsibilities now fall under the direction of the Bureau of Immigration and Customs Enforcement.

In February 2002, Indian immigrants filed a federal lawsuit against their former employer, the John Pickle Company of Tulsa, Oklahoma, alleging fraud, deceit, and civil rights violations. According to the suit's allegations, John Pickle, the owner of the equipment manufacturing company, hired 53 experienced Indian welders in October 2001. They had been recruited by a Mumbai employment agency called al-Samit, which required each man to borrow $2,500 at a high interest rate to pay an application fee. The new jobs promised $900 a

A Sikh (right) at work in the kitchen of an Indian restaurant in Burlington, Vermont. Many undocumented immigrants from India endure unfair working conditions and do not report them for fear that their undocumented status will be discovered by the authorities.

month with overtime pay, wage raises, and good benefits. At the promised salary, the workers expected they would quickly pay off the debt and be able to support their extended families back in India.

However, upon boarding the plane the new employees were told they would have a temporary "business visit" visa instead of one that was more permanent. Also, the immigrants claimed that Pickle's wife took their passports and visas and that Pickle put them on a grueling work schedule with poor living conditions. Their complaints were answered with threats of deportation. Some of the workers attempted an escape, but were found out and nearly deported, before the INS intervened to protect them. The welders remained in Tulsa, accepting the housing assistance and food from individuals and local charities. Meanwhile, the Pickle Company denied wrongdoing, claiming it had provided clean living quarters, Indian cuisine, and an open worksite. The Equal Employment Opportunity Commission picked up the case and filed an employment discrimination lawsuit in January 2003, which was still pending as of this writing.

7 FUTURE IMMIGRATION

In 2000 the U.S. Census reported that the country's total population stood at more than 281 million, with 1,678,765 Indian Americans making up about 0.6 percent of the population. The total of people of Indian descent living in the U.S. increased by 106 percent between 1990 and 2000. Canada's total population in 2001 was more than 30 million, with an estimated 314,000 Indians making up roughly 1 percent of the population. They made up the second-largest group of immigrants behind the Chinese.

The immigration numbers from India to North America could remain high in the future. Much depends on what the future of India brings. Will a good Indian economy create more job opportunities at home? Several American companies have already established operations in India, as the Internet has made telecommuting possible between the two countries.

On the other hand, if conditions should worsen at home, Indians may continue to seek new opportunities elsewhere. They may already have relatives in North America and want to follow in their footsteps. Changes in the North American economy is also a factor to consider. Will conditions in the United States and Canada continue to promise a better life? Also, how difficult will new restrictions make it for immigrants entering the country? Will they feel welcome?

◀ A Kashmiri woman consoles another woman after an unidentified youth is found dead in the streets of Srinagar, Kashmir, in April 2002. It is likely the ongoing ethnic conflicts in Kashmir and regions bordering Pakistan and Bangladesh will influence many Indians' decision to immigrate to the United States and Canada.

Prejudice and Hate Crimes

Some people fear that changes since the September 2001 terrorist attacks have made the country less hospitable to immigrants. Many Indian Americans have feared being mistaken as Middle Eastern, like the hijackers, and becoming the target of hate crimes. This fear was intensified in the days and weeks after the attacks. Sikhs in New York State distributed leaflets explaining their religion and culture, and Prime Minister Vajpayee of India asked President Bush to ensure the safety of

Indian American Legislator

Dalip Singh Saund, a Sikh, scaled many hurdles to become the first Asian American member of Congress. The son of an illiterate contractor, he was born September 20, 1899, in Amritsar, located in northern India. Appalled to see Indian soldiers massacre civilians in 1919, he left the country and immigrated to the United States in 1920. Saund arrived with a bachelor's degree, and went on to complete two master's degrees and a doctorate at the University of California.

Settling in Imperial Valley, California, Saund found success both at ranching and in business, manufacturing, and selling chemical fertilizer. He shed his outward identity as a Sikh by shaving his beard, removing his turban, and eventually marrying a Czech American. Saund addressed local Democratic groups about India and political issues, but laws barring Asians from citizenship prevented him from running for office.

In 1942, Saund founded the Indian Association of America, which lobbied for a bill to grant citizenship to Indians. The bill passed in 1946, and in 1949 Saund became a citizen. In 1950, he was elected Westmoreland Judicial District judge, but was denied the position because he had been a citizen for less than one year. Reelected in 1951, he served as judge until 1957.

In 1956, California's Fourth District Court of Appeals rejected a petition to block Saund from running for Congress because he had been a citizen for less than seven years. He won a seat in the 29th Congressional District. In his first term, he was appointed to the House Foreign Affairs Committee. Over three terms through 1962, he worked to improve relations between the United States and India. A stroke prevented him from running for a fourth term. He died April 23, 1973, at the age of 73.

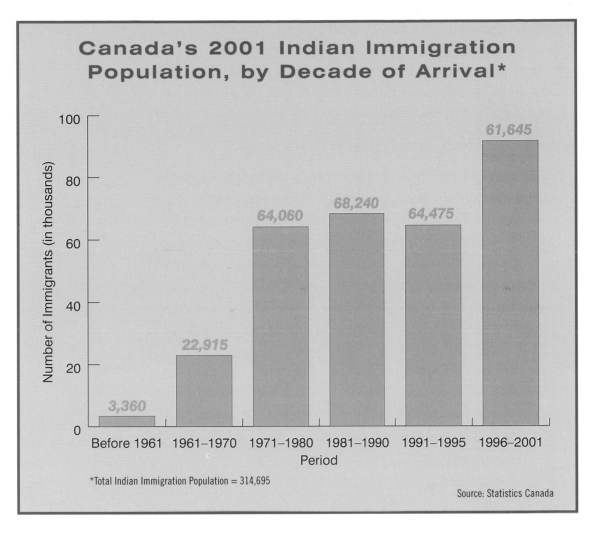

Canada's 2001 Indian Immigration Population, by Decade of Arrival*

Number of Immigrants (in thousands)

100

80

60

40

20

0

Before 1961 — 3,360

1961–1970 — 22,915

1971–1980 — 64,060

1981–1990 — 68,240

1991–1995 — 64,475

1996–2001 — 61,645

Period

*Total Indian Immigration Population = 314,695

Source: Statistics Canada

Sikhs living in the United States.

Sikhnet.com, a website source for the international Sikh community, reported 133 incidences of hate crime and harassment against Sikhs in the six short days following the attacks. A Hindu temple in Matawan, New Jersey, was firebombed in the wake of the attack. What was perhaps the most widely discussed attack occurred on September 15, 2001, four days after the terrorist attacks, in Mesa, Arizona. An Indian Sikh, Balbir Singh Sodhi, was killed outside the gas station he owned. The man who was charged for the attack told police he shot Sodhi because he wore a turban.

In the months after the attack, many Americans showed their

support for the Sikh victims of hate crimes. The Mesa community expressed its sympathy to the Sodhi family for their loss. On September 11, 2002, a year after the attacks, the Mesa Fire Department Honor Guard and the mayor of the city held a tribute for Sodhi, which was attended by his family.

Immigration and the Economy

A 2002 report by the Aspen Institute's Domestic Strategy Group predicts that immigration will be an important factor in maintaining healthy U.S. economic growth. The Aspen Institute report predicts that a decrease in the U.S. population and education levels will slow the country's economic growth.

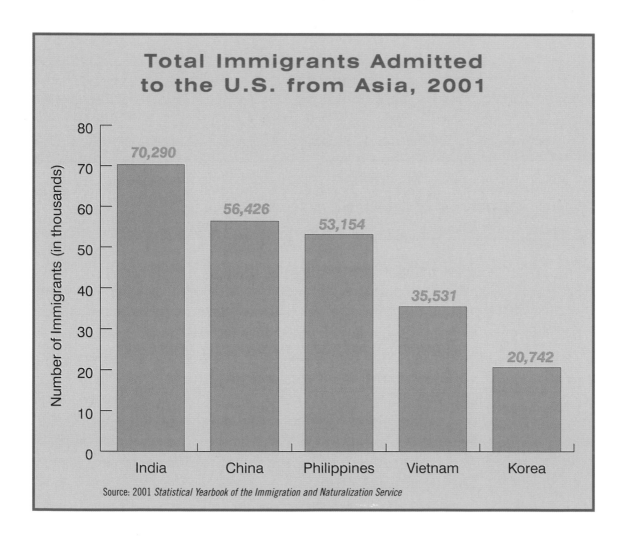

Total Immigrants Admitted to the U.S. from Asia, 2001

Source: 2001 *Statistical Yearbook of the Immigration and Naturalization Service*

In the future, industries will continue to need immigrant workers. Particular fields that will need skilled and educated workers are medicine, nursing, and high technology, a business field that employs large numbers of Indians. The National Center for Education Statistics has made similar predictions about the need for teachers in the future. Their reports estimate that by 2010 over 2 million teachers will be needed to teach students in the United States, and some education experts believe that this is yet another reason for increased immigration levels from India and other countries.

The significant impact in North America made by Indian entrepreneurs, engineers, and doctors in their respective fields is remarkable. Seeking to make better lives for themselves and their children, these immigrants have compiled a record of achievement that few could have imagined. And their futures remain bright. While the numbers of Indian immigrants are lower than those of other immigrant groups, their individual success stories show that a nation of immigrants is built one person at a time.

Famous Indian Americans/Canadians

Jagdish Bhagwati (1934–), noted economist from Columbia University who has published many significant works on international trade and economics.

G. S. Sharat Chandra (1938–2000), poet, translator, and fiction writer nominated for the Pulitzer Prize; literary journals such as the *Paris Review* and the *Missouri Review* have published his poems, many of which deal with the Indian immigrant experience.

Dr. Subrahmanyan Chandrasekhar (1910–95), astrophysicist and winner of the Nobel Prize in Physics in 1983. He discovered a phenomenon of stars that became known as the "Chandrasekhar limit"; the Chandra X-Ray telescope, used by NASA, is named after him.

Kalpana Chawla (1961–), aeronautical engineer and astronaut; became the first Indian American woman in space by serving as mission specialist aboard Space Shuttle Columbia Flight STS-87 in 1997.

Deepak Chopra (1947–), best-selling author and lecturer whose theories blending Western science with ayurveda gained popularity in the 1990s; founded the Center for Well Being in La Jolla, California.

Herb Dhaliwal (1952–), Canadian minister of natural resources, first person of South Asian descent appointed to a cabinet in a Western democracy when he was appointed minister of national revenue in 1998.

Ujjal Dosanjh (1947–), Indian Canadian lawyer and politician; became Canada's first provincial premier of Indian descent when he was elected premier of British Columbia in 2000.

Dinesh D'Souza (1961–), best-selling author, journalist, and political scientist; served during the Ronald Reagan administration as senior White House domestic policy analyst (1987–88); wrote *Ronald Reagan: How an Ordinary Man Became an Extraordinary Leader,* published in 1997.

Vinod Khosla (1955–), cofounder of Sun Microsystems, a large technology company based in Silicon Valley, California. He also serves on the board of directors of several other companies.

Zubin Mehta (1936–), orchestra conductor born in Mumbai. He has held positions as the musical director of the Montreal Symphony, Los Angeles Philharmonic Orchestra, New York Philharmonic, and the Israel Philharmonic, for whom he became Music Director for Life in 1981.

Famous Indian Americans/Canadians

Manoj Night Shyamalan (1970–), screenwriter and director, born in Pondicherry to physicians who immigrated to the United States. His most successful films include *The Sixth Sense* (1999) and *Signs* (2002).

Menaka Thakkar (1942–), dancer, choreographer, artistic director, and teacher. Master of the Bharatanyam, Odissi, and Kuchipudi Indian classical dance forms, she founded Nrtyakala: The Canadian Academy of Indian Dance in 1974.

Tanjore Viswanathan (1927–2002), flutist and music professor, first Indian musician named a national heritage fellow by the National Endowment for the Arts. He is also founder of the Navaratri Festival, which features Indian dance and music.

Fareed Zakaria (1965–), political scientist and editor of *Newsweek International*; former editor of *Foreign Affairs Quarterly*; received the South Asian Journalists Association's 2001 Journalism Leader Award for his contributions to international news coverage.

GLOSSARY

ashimsa—a deep religious reverence for life, with extreme avoidance of injuring living things.

ashram—a spiritual center, often used for yoga or other Hindu disciplines.

assimilation—the process of adopting characteristics of and being absorbed into a new culture.

bindi—a distinctive round red dot in the center of the forehead, usually signifying marriage in India.

Bollywood—a thriving film industry based in India.

caste—social position or class assigned at birth in the Hindu religion.

deportation—forced removal of someone from a country, usually back to his or her native land.

diaspora—the scattering of people who live outside their native country.

Diwali—Festival of Lights celebrating the victory of good over evil and the beginning of the new year.

eugenics—the study, now derided as a false science, of attempting to "improve" the human race through breeding; often used as a cover for racial discrimination.

globalization—closer connections across international borders.

gross national product (GNP)—an economic term that measures the total value of domestic goods and services produced by a country within the course of a year, including income flowing in from foreign countries.

mehndi—ancient henna tattoo body art.

mela—a large social gathering or a feast of Indian foods.

rangoli—art from natural materials such as rice, flower petals, or tinted rice flour.

refugee—an alien outside the United States who is unable or unwilling to return to his or her country of nationality because of persecution or a well-founded fear of persecution.

GLOSSARY

sari—a traditional woman's garment consisting of nearly seven yards of fabric wrapped around the body.

swami—a Hindu religious teacher.

visa—official authorization that permits arrival at a port of entry but does not guarantee admission into the United States.

FURTHER READING

Chandra, G. S. Sharat. *Sari of the Gods*. Minneapolis, Minn.: Coffee House Press, 1998.

Chandra, Vikram. *Red Earth and Pouring Rain*. New York: Little, Brown & Co., 1997.

Dasgupta, Shamita Das, ed. *A Patchwork Shawl: Chronicles of South Asian Women.* New Brunswick, N.J.: Rutgers University Press, 1998.

Divakaruni, Chitra Banerjee. *Arranged Marriage: Stories.* New York: Anchor, 1996.

D'Souza, Dinesh. *What's So Great About America*. Washington, D.C: Regnery Publishing, 2002.

Foner, Nancy. *From Ellis Island to JFK: New York's Two Great Waves of Immigration*. New Haven, Conn.: Yale University Press, 2002.

Kamdar, Mira. *Motiba's Tattoos: A Granddaughter's Journey into Her Indian Family's Past*. New York: Plume, 2000.

Lahiri, Jhumpa. *Interpreter of Maladies*. Boston: Houghton Mifflin, 2000.

Segal, Uma A. *A Framework for Immigration: Applications to Asians in the United States.* New York: Columbia University Press, 2002.

INTERNET RESOURCES

http://www.bcis.gov

The website of the Bureau of Citizenship and Immigration Services explains the various functions of the organization and provides specific information on immigration policy.

http://www.canadianhistory.ca/iv/main.html

This site contains an excellent history of immigration to Canada from the 1800s to the present.

http://www.garamchai.com/index.html

A collection of links to Indian American associations, publications, temples, churches, mosques, and other websites of interest.

http://www.indiacurrents.com/

A monthly publication covering the topics of literature, dance, music, and film that are of interest to Indian Americans.

http://www.indiatribune.com/

The companion website of the weekly newspaper for Indian Americans that is published in Chicago, New York, and Atlanta.

http://www.indiawest.com/

A weekly Indian American newsmagazine featuring coverage of events and developments in India.

http://www.indius.org/

Indian Americans Involved in the U.S (IndiUS) is a forum created to share news and articles that promote the culture of Indian Americans and encourage community involvement.

INTERNET RESOURCES

http://www.littleindia.com/

A monthly feature magazine with articles on Indian life outside of India.

http://www.newsindia-times.com/

A New York–based newspaper reporting on issues of interest to the Indian community.

http://www.rediff.com

A media and Internet company with comprehensive resources for the Indian American community.

http://www.iado.org

The homesite of the Indo-American Democratic Organization (IADO), a lobby group that serves Indian Americans and is engaged in issues concerning them, including immigration, education, and hate crimes.

INDEX

Numbers in **bold italic** refer to captions.

INDEX

INDEX

INDEX

PICTURE CREDITS

CONTRIBUTORS

SENATOR EDWARD M. KENNEDY has represented Massachusetts in the United States Senate for more than 40 years. Kennedy serves on the Senate Judiciary Committee, where he is the senior Democrat on the Immigration Subcommittee. He currently is the ranking member on the Health, Education, Labor and Pensions Committee in the Senate, and also serves on the Armed Services Committee, where he is a member of the Senate Arms Control Observer Group. He is also a member of the Congressional Friends of Ireland and a trustee of the John F. Kennedy Center for the Performing Arts in Washington, D.C.

Throughout his career, Kennedy has fought for issues that benefit the citizens of Massachusetts and the nation, including the effort to bring quality health care to every American, education reform, raising the minimum wage, defending the rights of workers and their families, strengthening the civil rights laws, assisting individuals with disabilities, fighting for cleaner water and cleaner air, and protecting and strengthening Social Security and Medicare for senior citizens.

Kennedy is the youngest of nine children of Joseph P. and Rose Fitzgerald Kennedy, and is a graduate of Harvard University and the University of Virginia Law School. His home is in Hyannis Port, Massachusetts, where he lives with his wife, Victoria Reggie Kennedy, and children, Curran and Caroline. He also has three grown children, Kara, Edward Jr., and Patrick, and four grandchildren.

Senior consulting editor STUART ANDERSON served as Executive Associate Commissioner for Policy and Planning and Counselor to the Commissioner at the Immigration and Naturalization Service from August 2001 until January 2003. He spent four and a half years on Capitol Hill on the Senate Immigration Subcommittee, first for Senator Spencer Abraham and then as Staff Director of the subcommittee for Senator Sam Brownback. Prior to that, he was Director of Trade and Immigration Studies at the Cato Institute in Washington, D.C., where he produced reports on the history of immigrants in the military and the role of immigrants in high technology. He currently serves as Executive Director of the National Foundation for American Policy, a nonpartisan public policy research organization focused on trade, immigration, and international relations. He has an M.A. from Georgetown University and a B.A. in Political Science from Drew University. His articles have appeared in such publications as the *Wall Street Journal*, *New York Times*, and *Los Angeles Times*.

MARIAN L. SMITH served as the senior historian of the U.S. Immigration and Naturalization Service (INS) from 1988 to 2003, and is currently the immigration and naturalization historian within the Department of Homeland Security in Washington, D.C. She studies, publishes, and speaks on the history of the immigration agency and is active in the management of official 20th-century immigration records.

PETER HAMMERSCHMIDT is the First Secretary (Financial and Military Affairs) for the Permanent Mission of Canada to the United Nations. Before taking this position, he was a ministerial speechwriter and policy specialist for the Department of National

CONTRIBUTORS

Defence in Ottawa. Prior to joining the public service, he served as the Publications Director for the Canadian Institute of Strategic Studies in Toronto. He has a B.A. (Honours) in Political Studies from Queen's University, and an MScEcon in Strategic Studies from the University of Wales, Aberystwyth. He currently lives in New York, where in his spare time he operates a freelance editing and writing service, Wordschmidt Communications.

Manuscript reviewer ESTHER OLAVARRIA serves as General Counsel to Senator Edward M. Kennedy, ranking Democrat on the U.S. Senate Judiciary Committee, Subcommittee on Immigration. She is Senator Kennedy's primary advisor on immigration, nationality, and refugee legislation and policies. Prior to her current job, she practiced immigration law in Miami, Florida, working at several nonprofit organizations. She cofounded the Florida Immigrant Advocacy Center and served as managing attorney, supervising the direct service work of the organization and assisting in the advocacy work. She also worked at Legal Services of Greater Miami, as the directing attorney of the American Immigration Lawyers Association Pro Bono Project, and at the Haitian Refugee Center, as a staff attorney. She clerked for a Florida state appellate court after graduating from the University of Florida Law School. She was born in Havana, Cuba, and raised in Florida.

Reviewer JANICE V. KAGUYUTAN is Senator Edward M. Kennedy's advisor on immigration, nationality, and refugee legislation and policies. Prior to working on Capitol Hill, Ms. Kaguyutan was a staff attorney at the NOW Legal Defense and Education Fund's Immigrant Women Program. Ms. Kaguyutan has written and trained extensively on the rights of immigrant victims of domestic violence, sexual assault, and human trafficking. Her previous work includes representing battered immigrant women in civil protection order, child support, divorce, and custody hearings, as well as representing immigrants before the Immigration and Naturalization Service on a variety of immigration matters.

A former newspaper reporter, JAN MCDANIEL is the author of more than 20 novels and nonfiction books. She has a master's degree from Texas A&M University and lives in Chattanooga, Tennessee.

DATE DUE